Inside Russia

The life and times of
Zoya Zarubina

For the first time
a female Soviet intelligence officer
tells her story of life, love, and
triumph over personal tragedy

by Inez Cope Jeffery, Ph.D.

*Dear Lucille — we wish
you enjoyable reading!*

Inez Cope Jeffery

Zoya Zarubina

EAKIN PRESS ⟡ Austin, Texas

FIRST EDITION

Copyright © 1999
By Inez Cope Jeffery, Ph.D.

Published in the United States of America
By Eakin Press
An Imprint of Sunbelt Media, Inc.
P.O. Drawer 90159 ★ Austin, TX 78709-0159
email: eakinpub@sig.net
website: www.eakinpress.com

Edited by
Boris Krouse
Melissa Locke Roberts,
Senior Editor

ALL RIGHTS RESERVED.

ISBN 1-57168-309-7

Library of Congress Cataloging-in-Publication Data

Jeffery, Inez Cope.
    Russia, an inside view : the life & times of Dr. Zoya Zarubina / by Inez Cope
Jeffery.
        p.   cm.
    Includes bibliographical references and index.
    ISBN 1-57168-309-7
    1. Zarubina, Zoya Vasilyevna. 2. Translators—Soviet Union—Biography. 3. Soviet
Union—History—1925-1953. 4. Soviet Union—History—1953-1995. I. Title.
    DK268.Z34J44   1999
    947.08'092—dc21
    [B]   99-12724
                                                                                      CIP

Contents

Foreword

THIS BOOK IS AN inspired collaboration between two remarkable women: Zoya Zarubina, its subject, and Inez Jeffery, its author. It results from the more than thirty trips through Russia taken by Dr. Inez C. Jeffery in company with Dr. Zoya Zarubina during the past thirty years, and from the international conferences which they have chaired together. From their moments of reflection and private discussion during these conferences come echoes of their common devotion to the dream of a better world. Resolving to tell Zoya's story as an expression of this dream, they have done so in an objective and evenhanded narrative, but not in any way a dispassionate one.

A passionate commitment to human justice and love is always just beneath the surface of the text. *Inside Russia* is a testimony to the spirit and commitment of a gallant woman, maintaining her ideals of compassion and world peace despite hardships and betrayals. Too often the sacrifices made by women have been untold and thus lost from human memory. Too often the spotlight has been on conspicuous deeds of derring-do, on feats of battlefield bravery or political skill. Rarely has it illuminated the quiet heroism of women locked in day-to-day combat with evil—with the "Infame" of Voltaire, yet holding fast to their ideals.

Compromises . . . yes. One does not live in a viciously depersonalized society without making concessions, if only to save the lives of those whom one loves. All the more so for Zoya Zarubina, who at the most desperate time in her life and in the life of Mother Russia, often went hungry herself as she worked twenty-hour days to feed an extended family of six. For those of us who have some knowledge of the hardships endured by the Russians during World

War II and its aftermath, and some appreciation of the Russian "soul" and indomitable spirit, labels are misleading. Having taught in Russian universities and institutes before the end of Communism, I have experienced its rigid controls on education and the search for Truth. Yet, even with those strictures, Zoya Zarubina exemplified the compelling mission of a teacher: To use one's personal talents and gifts as a touchstone to bring out the hidden potential in each individual—thus, eventually, to bring about change. Russian acquaintances who studied under Zoya when she was Dean at the Linguistics Institute assert that she was, indeed, "one of the good guys!"

Such she has been, throughout her career as teacher, linguist, interpreter, and advocate for peace. Serving under Stalin, Zoya was the young hostess for Roosevelt in Tehran and for Churchill in Yalta, as well as one of the interpreters at Potsdam. As the head interpreter of all Communist Party Congresses and, for ten years, of the Soviet delegation to the Conference on Security and Cooperation in Europe, Zoya was in Helsinki at the signing of the Helsinki Accords. She has served as Dean of the English Language Department at Moscow's prestigious Foreign Language Institute (now University), and taught for twenty-five years at the diplomatic Academy of the Ministry of Foreign Affairs in Moscow. Among her many unofficial functions, she has long been a mainstay of the diplomatic community in Moscow. More recently she has been Russia's delegate to international conferences on ethnic strife, and has been actively engaged in creating a political women's caucus in Russia. She is the founder of International Educators for Peace and Understanding and has spoken throughout the world on behalf of the role of educators as a bridge between peoples and cultures. More than anything else, perhaps, this is the mission which has defined Zoya's life. In her own words, published in *Teacher, the Teachers' Union Herald*, February-March 1996, "The most important thing in teaching is to convey to students how to love others."

Zoya Zarubina has been a role model of this, her stated professional priority. I have been with her at educational and professional conferences, here and in the Russia. Usually she has been the indefatigable impresario, orchestrating everything to perfection. But whether leader or simply a participant, she has generously drawn on her wide acquaintances and on the loyalties of her friends to help supply the needs of the organizing committee. Herself a quintessential diplomat, Zoya seemed always able to coax, cajole, command, pull strings, and add a stress-relieving dose of humor when appropriate.

. . . And, of course, interpreted. Sitting in the front row while Zoya interpreted the conference proceedings, I listened with amazement. She skipped over the sections which she considered unimportant and freely interpreted the rest, fixing me with a stern glance, but also a barely perceptible twinkle. Clearly she was saying, "Don't tell on me! We have to get through this summary quickly!" Most of the omissions, in fact, were immaterial, and a few were made for the sake of diplomacy and tact.

The Life and Times of Dr. Zoya Zarubina is unique because Zoya is unique—in her loyalty to Mother Russia and to humankind. Her wide experience of living abroad and of assimilating, then teaching, other cultures has made her at home wherever she is. Her life has been a world apart from the experiences of most middle Americans, yet her perspective is universal. Zoya Zarubina is universally admired and respected for her expertise in many fields, for the talents which she has used to the advantage of others, and for her myriad accomplishments. But it is her sensitivity, spirit, and vision which have linked her to friends worldwide—to all who identify with her in a commonality of shared hopes and dreams for a humane world society of justice and peace.

ANN L. COPPLE, PH.D.
January 29, 1999

Preface

THE THINKING OF Middle America has been held captive by misinformation disseminated by national leaders and the media about the Soviet Union and Russia for more than seventy years. School books revealed little about the big experiment in socialism. At the same time Soviet leaders also told their people what to think about Americans. Little wonder that both sides had all the information they needed to see each other as enemies. They were different and we were critical. We were capitalists and they gave it the face of evil. Because of misunderstanding and a lack of good will on the part of national leaders on both sides, the Cold War created a blockade to the exchange of ideas and information. When communication ceases, mystery deepens, and the middle ground of compromise disappears.

Since 1967 I have been going to the Soviet Union and Russia every year and at times, two and three times a year. Educators enjoyed going to the Russian Winter Festival, and most of the time we could get several lecturers from the Academy of Pedagogical Sciences to talk about their educational system, even though it was the winter vacation.

At other times our hosts took the group to many different areas of the Soviet Union for educational seminars with the members of the Academy of Pedagogical Sciences and The Teachers' Trade Union. Local teachers would join us. It was difficult to answer questions about American education because participants came from many different states. Our answers to their questions would be challenged within our own group since each state has its own educational plan. Teachers from Alma Ata, Bratsk, Irkutsk, Novosibirsk, Tashkent, Samarkand, and other cities with Asian population would have the same answers to questions that we heard in Moscow and St. Petersburg (Leningrad) because the one right answer came from Moscow.

Our American dilemma disturbed the Soviets because they wondered how we could educate our children to be good patriots. They questioned our lack of a national plan. They accepted the system as it came from Moscow where it had been approved by the Central Committee of the Communist Party. Arguments among Americans about differences from state to state gave the Soviet teachers a sense of security about their system of education—they knew no other.

Working with large groups of educators made me aware that our experience was different from that described by our esteemed American Sovietologists, some of whom were well-read, but had limited association with the people of the Soviet Union. Even though they were intellectuals, some were obviously prejudiced. It was disturbing to me that our top national leaders were accepting their suggestions and advice and acting upon it.

There were problems and frustrations with the seminars, but we were involved with the people—Russians, Asians, and the many ethnic groups living across the eleven time zones. We were permitted to go into most areas of the Soviet Union and Mongolia.

Dr. Gerald Read of Kent State University (Ohio) worked diligently to clear the way for American educators to share experiences with Soviet educators. One of his contacts was Dr. Zoya Zarubina. I was, for a number of years, liaison for The Delta Kappa Gamma Society International for his seminars and hundreds of our members participated. These teachers had a personal relationship with other cultures that they could share with their students to broaden their perception.

There were seventy in each seminar group. They were classroom teachers, superintendents, principals, and school board members. For the Russian Winter Festival there would be as many as 180 participants.

My work with Dr. Read ended in 1978. I was, however, inspired and pushed by my friend, Madge Rudd, who went on every trip to the Soviet Union until she was ninety-one, to continue to take other groups of educators and interested Americans. I believed then, and still do, that the solution to problems between the two countries can better be solved by people to people association and understanding. Madge shared my belief that American and Soviet educators in cooperation could tear down the walls that divided us. She was a conservative, but she spent her ninetieth birthday in the Soviet Union supporting this belief.

Zoya Zarubina was always careful (as she had to be in the early years), yet more relaxed than other Soviet educators. She seemed more sure of herself. Representing the academicians of her country, she had to reflect the philosophy of the national leaders, but she did it with charm and a sense of humor. We met her when she was volunteering at Friendship House in Moscow.

In the spring of 1992 I met her again when I was with a group of Delta Kappa Gamma members at a meeting of the Women's Committee. Her world had changed, and as we sat together at the speaker's table, she spoke frankly and openly about issues we had been wondering about for years, but could never get definitive answers. During our conversation she agreed to come to Texas in the fall of 1992 for speaking engagements. From Texas she went to Virginia to speak to a group of Delta Kappa Gamma members in a regional meeting.

We talked a lot about writing the story of her exceptionally interesting and involved life, but so much of it was painful to remember, and she had to think about it. She returned for lectures in 1994, then came back in September of 1995 to stay six months and record her story. The recording and writing has been exciting, emotionally draining, and at times painful because she had never revealed her involvement with world affairs from 1940 to the present, including her experience while translating the Atomic Bomb papers as a military intelligence officer. Not even the members of her family knew what was entailed in her assignments.

This story is for Middle America in the hope that personal and professional sharing will strike a note of accord thereby helping more of us understand how alike we are in family problems, ambitions, desires, loves, sorrows, and limitations. Due to political constraints we have not been permitted to share our personal experiences.

As an interpreter fluent in English, French, German, and her native Russian, Zoya has been in the inner sanctum of summit meetings which have affected the course of history. Her experiences range from Tehran, Yalta, Potsdam, and the Nuremberg trials through the meetings of the Conference on Security and Cooperation in Europe which started in 1972 and continued to the signing of the Helsinki Accords on August 1, 1975. While working with the interpreters from the countries involved in the conference, she came to understand the way leaders of other countries think and express their beliefs and wishes. She also recognized that those designated to represent her country were not always well informed about global issues.

Interpreters hear the words and sometimes feel the heartbeat of the world leaders who speak at international conferences. Zoya Zarubina is a sensitive and compassionate woman who has lived under constraint for many years, daring only to function as she was directed in order to protect her family.

As a school girl she lived in a KGB apartment complex where leaders in the KGB and the military were being taken away on Stalin's orders and never returned. The purges came in waves, and everybody felt them. There was no way of predicting who might be next.

The KGB provided the best school for the children of intelligence and military officers. The young students had many opportunities to expand their activities through Pioneer Camps. Zoya was an athlete with many interests that kept her involved in a variety of endeavors. She excelled in public speaking and was often the student designated to thank the KGB leaders for special activities before the students would perform for them.

This is the story of a Russian woman who was involved in history as it unfolded from World War II (The Great Patriotic War) to the present. For twenty-eight years prior to 1998 she worked for the Diplomatic Academy of The Ministry of Foreign Affairs and prepared diplomats to live in other countries, taught languages, and represented her country as an interpreter and/or delegate to international meetings. At the age of seventy-nine she is still active with the Academy.

She worked with peace movements as soon as she could and since *Perestroika* has organized the International Movement of Educators for Peace and Understanding and serves as the vice-president.

Her second marriage was to Bernard Cooper, an American who moved to the Soviet Union with his parents when he was sixteen. He was a bench interpreter during the Nuremberg Trials, where she met him for the first time. Later he was a sports commentator on Moscow radio. Through her interest in sports they renewed their acquaintance at the radio station, and it turned into a serious relationship. When Zoya's assignments took her out of the country, he called and wrote to her every day. His letters always ended with, "Love forever and ever and even after," a phrase Zoya has adapted to express her deep and abiding love for Bernie and her devotion and patriotic loyalty to her country.

INEZ COPE JEFFERY

Acknowledgments

IT TAKES MANY cooperative friends and associates to make the completion of any major project possible. This was the first time Zoya Zarubina had looked back over her life and then agreed to record it. She traveled from Moscow to Austin, Texas, and I sat with her for thirty-two hours of recording, encouraging her, and asking questions. At times she became very emotional, and the scene became a bit turbulent as she approached some of the more tragic and unfair moments. But she realized that the story must be told. I admire her ability to tell the story in a straightforward manner especially since she was trained and conditioned for the Intelligence service in the Soviet military.

Special appreciation is extended to the many friends who helped transcribe the story from recordings to paper. It was a tedious job, but they seemed to enjoy what they heard. Kelly Crews not only did some of the transcribing, but stood by to help with some major problems a novice can have with a computer. I am very grateful to her for responding to calls at a late hour and for having a serene disposition.

Several persons brought in resource material which was not readily available. We want them to know we appreciate all of the historical information, even though they prefer not to be named.

I could not have completed this project without the unselfish hours of work my daughter, Jan Harris, put in at any time of day or night. She worked many hours at the computer and ran errands when necessary. It is a blessing to have someone willing and available who is talented and practical.

Vi Marie Taylor and Lynn Cooksey encouraged me to talk with Ed Eakin, Austin publisher. After talking too long with agents who wanted specific things just their way, visiting with Ed gave me new hope, and things began to move smoothly. An understanding publisher is a blessed asset.

Last but not least, Sam Williams and Alexander Rodriguez were willing to come promptly in response to every SOS when the computer failed to respond to the conscientious efforts of a novice. To them—my forever gratitude!

INEZ COPE JEFFERY

Introduction

DAUGHTER OF VASILY ZARUBIN (a.k.a. Zubilin) and step-daughter of Naum Eitingon (Leonid Naumov), both well-known Soviet intelligence officers, Zoya Vasilyevna Zarubina was born and grew up in a minefield of opportunity, privilege, and despair. But her heritage led her into excitement, adventure, risk, and responsibility. She lived in change and uncertainty during World War II (The Great Patriotic War) and was proud to serve her country in any capacity.

Loyalty to and love for her family motivated her and during the twelve years of Eitingon's prison sentence, starting in 1951, she was the sole means of support for ten family members, including two children of his extended family. While still in her early twenties, she was given the responsibility of taking part in the preparation, physical arrangements, and security for the Tehran Conference. She then served as liaison between the different delegations at Yalta and Potsdam. She was hostess for the summit meetings and also worked as an interpreter and translator. She is fluent in English, German, and French, as well as Russian, and retains some Chinese and Turkish from her experience as a child in those countries.

Zoya's interest in and awareness of the importance of languages started when she was six years of age in Peking, China, where she attended an American school while Eitingon was on assignment. There was no Soviet school in the Soviet Embassy in those days so she attended an American school and became fluent in English. Playing with her American friends extended her vocabulary. When her sister, Svetlana, was born, the Chinese *amah* spoke only Chinese, and Zoya's mother spoke only Russian, so she learned Chinese to interpret for her mother. Zoya was a precocious child, and her ability to interpret from one language to another started at age five in the American school. At age seven she was learning a third language in order to help her mother who had become very frustrated when attempting to communicate with the Chinese cook and the *amah* after the baby was born. Little wonder that some of the most exciting moments of her life, and the experiences from which she learned about the rest of the world, came because of her skill as interpreter.

The Turkish she learned coincidentally during her stay in Turkey as a member of Leonid Eitingon's family when he went there on special assignment. This posting included reporting on the activities of Trotsky. Zoya was privileged as long as Stalin recognized the devoted and patriotic service being given by her father and her stepfather who was Jewish. In the Soviet Union being a Jew was a nationality not a religion.

A skilled interpreter, Zoya has been in the inner sanctum of historical events as head interpreter for the Supreme Soviet. She supervised translation into sixteen languages while serving her country as an interpreter. She has also interpreted at the United Nations. Later, she established the first United Nations Language Training Center in the Soviet Union because translators and interpreters from English to Russian were very much in demand.

Her great desire for peace led her to join the USSR–Great Britain Friendship Group and the USSR–USA Friendship Groups and to organize the International Organization of Educators for Peace and Understanding. She served as interpreter for the Soviet Union during the working years of the Conference on Security and Cooperation in Europe which culminated the Helsinki Accords in 1975. She learned much about the rest of the world.

For thirty years Zoya has worked at the Diplomatic Academy of the Ministry of Foreign Affairs after being Dean of the English Department at the Institute of Foreign Languages. At the Academy she was a lecturer in the Department of Philosophy and Contemporary Ideological Problems. Training diplomats was a part of her job.

The secret service (military intelligence) has had several name changes from the time of its inception, but in this book it will be referred to as the KGB because that is its most familiar name. No effort is being made to base the information in this book on research. This is the story told by a woman whose life activities coincided with the forceful historical events that have changed the world over the past half century.

CHAPTER 1

The Tehran Conference
Tehran, Iran
November–December 1943

DURING WORLD WAR II plans were made to have Stalin, Roosevelt, and Churchill meet at the Soviet Embassy in Tehran and discuss important items about coordinating landings in Europe to open a second front and to continue with the Soviet offensive against Germany from the East. They were also to make an agreement about the Soviet entry into the war with Japan.

The Soviets had not been involved in high level international conferences abroad before and, since they were hosting this conference, there were many detailed plans that had to be put in place. In 1943, at the age of twenty-three, Zoya Zarubina was assigned to work in Iran with the Conference. Her superiors in Intelligence decided it was best if the Soviet Embassy did not know that she was a single woman because single women were not assigned abroad. At first they decided to forge a marriage, and the man they designated was her former pioneer leader Nikolai Skvortsov. He was not satisfied with the arrangement and talked her into actually marrying him. He was more persuasive when he told her that he knew her husband had been killed at the front since she separated from him so there was no reason why they could not make the marriage official.

She accepted the plan and had very little time to realize she was married. She learned later that he had lied to her about her husband's death. He even boasted to his friends that he would not have to take care of her child because it had two grandfathers who were high ranking intelligence officers. In Iran she worked officially in the Department of Information on the planning and preparation for some time before the conference. It turned out that she was to be a hostess. Since she already worked for Intelligence she was involved in furnishing the premises for the U.S. president and trying to arrange everything in an orderly and functional manner.

"In those days, unlike conferences today, we did not know his preferences in wallpaper color or the kind of furniture he preferred. It was a bit like a blind date—we just didn't know anything about President Roosevelt," Zoya said.

They could not buy new furniture because it would have aroused curiosity and broken confidentiality. Officials told Zoya that she could go to any room in the Embassy and take the furniture of her choice. She ordered Soviet officials to move furniture here and there until she felt that the rooms were balanced. All of them followed the orders because Beria, head of the KGB, told them that she was the boss, and that they were to follow whatever she instructed them to do because she was in charge of interior decorations. No one dared do other than what she instructed, regardless of their official status, because Beria had put her in charge.

When everything was settled, they got the list of American, British, and Soviet participants. Zoya found that she was also assigned to be a translator.

With the official number of participants identified, it was time to order the big conference table. Zoya and her husband went to a cabinet maker in the city and told him that they were going to get married. They had to have a very large table made for their wedding, and it had to be done quickly. Keeping plans secret for such a conference in a large, bustling Muslim city was a real accomplishment. When the table was delivered to the Embassy everyone was surprised—such a large table for such a young couple! Not all of the employees in the Embassy knew what was being planned. Zoya now says, "Three weeks before I was to leave for the United States in

1995 I went to the memorial in Moscow which was set up to celebrate the fiftieth anniversary of the victory in World War II, and to my amazement, I saw the table as one of the exhibits. It was a different color—the top was covered with dark mahogany paint, but the legs were the original color.

"After the table was set up in the Embassy [in 1943], during the night we checked the complete lists of those who would participate. In those days there were no security pass tags to identify participants so I was posted at the gate. The security guards were in civilian clothes standing at the entrance gate to the Embassy. Their orders were, 'When the lady says open the gate—open the gate!' Everything was being done very secretly because there were still rumors that the Germans knew the conference was to be held so it was necessary to be on the alert every second.

"That night I was writing ID cards from the lists given us by the U.S. delegation. I asked, 'How can I identify their faces?' The security officer said, 'Stupid, if it is your handwriting on the card, the face doesn't matter.' They had been warned that I would be checking them in. Later on I learned to know them by name and face. Two of the people I came to know and have met several times in the years following were Mr. Averell Harriman and Mr. Llewelyn Thompson. Mr. Thompson later became the United States ambassador to the Soviet Union sometime in the 60s."

The time came for the large delegation to arrive, and Zoya was summoned to Mr. Molotov's office. She was told to call the military airfield and, in code, ask whether the United States president and his party had landed safely. She called and found out that they had arrived. Admiral Leahy came to the phone. Zoya asked him in a coded message if they were coming to the Embassy. Admiral Leahy said, "No, we will come tomorrow morning."

"Mr. Molotov was sitting nearby listening to the conversation. When he heard they were not coming he flew into a rage and said, 'What do you think you are doing? Who the hell are you anyway? Who commissioned you to do this job? Are you quite sure of what they said? What am I going to say to Stalin?' I told him that he had also heard the message. So I asked the gentleman on the phone to come to the Embassy and explain things to Molotov because Stalin was expecting President Roosevelt. Molotov turned to me and said, 'You had better see that they do come!'

"Some time passed and Admiral Leahy and General Marshall arrived at the Embassy. I was doing the interpreting and they said, 'You see, the American people will not understand if the President goes immediately to the Soviet Embassy. He will stay at the Mission tonight, and he will come to the Embassy tomorrow morning.'"

The Soviet and British Embassies were very close by. It was just a matter of crossing the road to get to the Soviet Embassy where the conference was being held for the convenience of President Roosevelt. Winston Churchill could go out of the Embassy gate and into the Soviet Embassy gate. Sikh Indian guards were on duty at the British Embassy passage. The American Mission was on the other side of the city, and it would have been a security risk for the United States president to get across the city of Tehran several times a day. Precautions were very tight and, as host to the conference, the Soviets wanted no incident to occur during the visit of Americans and British.

"The first morning was very exciting for all of us. Beria placed me at the entrance gate and told security officers to follow my orders, and to open the gates when I gave the command. Periodically, the officers looked at passing cars and asked me to identify them so they could open the gate. I saw a jeep coming and could see GIs sitting at attention. I could tell by their uniforms that they were Americans so I said, 'Let them enter.' As they opened the gate, I had a moment of doubt—what if these were German paratroopers disguised as Americans! I put my foot on the running board of the jeep and ordered them to clear the main lane as I directed them to one side and ordered that they be kept there. I told the security officers to keep an eye on them. I was in a bit of a quandary because I knew I could not make a mistake. When I saw them chewing gum, I knew they were Americans.

"Other cars came in, and I kept checking the ID cards I had written. One big car was coming to the gate, and I would not let it through until I looked inside to check the passengers. It was President Roosevelt, and I was on the running board welcoming him to the Soviet Embassy. I rode with them to the main entrance. It was a long drive, and when I left them at the Embassy door, I had to run back to the gate. By the time I got back a number of American delegates were feverishly waiting in line for me to clear them with Soviet security."

Zoya was very young to have such heavy responsibilities and she was also the only woman on the team. "I was young and too excited to analyze the role I was playing. I felt honored to be doing the job. Many of the assignments were quite unexpected.

"I came into the conference hall whenever the deliberations were going on if I had a request that needed to be taken to the table. Only service people came in to bring whatever was needed by the delegates. But I saw and felt enough to realize what a long way we have come from that first conference to the conferences we now watch on television. Now everything is in place with all of the details worked out.

"When everything was ready for the first session in Tehran, we found out that we didn't have enough pencils. We put the paper around, but had no pencils to go with it. In those days there were no ball-point pens—only Parker ink pens and we Soviets did not have those, so generals were trying to round up pencils among themselves and get them sharpened.

"At the opening of the Conference, President Roosevelt was the first to preside. Everything moved very smoothly. Important talks took place at luncheons and dinners as well as at the conference table."

Zoya got a note from President Roosevelt's security that some Filipino boys would be coming and to let them in. She had no idea who Filipinos were or what they looked like so she asked security who they were, and what they were to do at the conference. The response was that they would be arriving in a pick-up truck to cook for the President. She let the truck through the gate, but carefully checked inside and found small dark men who did not look like any Americans she had ever seen. Since she didn't understand what Filipino meant she assumed that it was their code name, but there they were, these small dark men, getting out of the truck ready to unload things. She called the mansion and was instructed to clear them.

After the first luncheon given by President Roosevelt, Stalin said to him, "I was told that here in the Embassy there is a large man-size, pre-Revolutionary samovar. So I am going to invite you to have tea—Russian style." Stalin had been told about the samovar, but no one had tested it. It was in the basement directly below President Roosevelt's quarters. "Security men from the American side were in the basement so I went down with the Soviet generals.

I watched as the generals put wood into the bottom of the samovar to start the fire. When they lit it there was a sudden blast. It must have been clogged because no one had used it for years. It wasn't a very big blast but enough to scare everybody to death."

The invitation from Stalin was so unexpected, security did not have a chance to check it out. It was a close call. "Those incidents made us behave more humanly and reduced the tension.

"It seemed that I was in the jeep most of the time going back and forth between the gate and the mansion. I would no more than get to the mansion when I would be summoned back to the gate. It became very uncomfortable at times because there were no toilets at the gate. Now and then I would have to ask the jeep driver to get me to a toilet."

One day Zoya had to stay at the gate too long and got bored. She told the guards that she was a champion athlete. They challenged her to show them and pointed at a tree as a finish goal for her to run. She accepted the challenge and ran at her best toward the tree. When she was almost there, Beria stepped out from behind the tree. No one ever knew where this stern chief of the KGB would appear, but everyone immediately got back to their jobs.

Both American and Soviet security men were everywhere. Americans were shielding their president, and Soviets were behind every tree. Every effort was made to be sure that nothing interrupted the work being done.

"I did not know that Stalin was such a fragile, short man. He was no taller than I, and he had small-pox scars on his face. It was difficult to say what color his eyes were. Sometimes they even looked yellow. Other times they were dark, but in my limited experience with him, he never looked straight into my eyes. You always felt that he was listening very intently even in personal contacts when the conference was not in session. He was smoking most of the time.

"One of my encounters with Stalin was a near tragedy. I was in the main hall while the delegates were assembling. I was in a civilian suit and received orders to do an errand quickly. I turned to run to the jeep, and as I was going across the big hall, Mr. Churchill had already arrived. The delegates were milling around the table. Stalin always chose to come at the last moment. I worked my way through the hall at a very fast pace and ran down the marble steps to the huge entrance door.

"As I rushed down the steps I saw security men standing at attention, but I was in a hurry and kept going when suddenly a door opened at the bottom, and I hit someone on the shoulder. When I glanced at the shoulder stripes on his uniform I realized it was Generalissimus Stalin! I stood frozen—I thought they would surely shoot me on the spot. I stood at attention as three official delegates to Tehran passed by—Mr. Stalin; Mr. Molotov, Minister of Foreign Affairs; and Mr. Voroshilov, Minister of Defense. Mr. Voroshilov patted me on the hand and said, 'It's alright kid, it's alright!' I was really scared because I knew I gave Stalin a hard push while trying to hurry out of the building and get to the gate.

"There was a big dinner for the security and technical staffs at the conclusion of the conference. Wonderful food was served. Don't forget—this was in the midst of the war in 1943. At home rations were very limited, but for this dinner there was a variety of seafood and everything that went with it. A waiter came in with a tray of champagne and caviar. He said, 'This is for the lady from the grateful gentleman whom you did not knock off his feet totally!' I blushed and realized that the security officers had all seen my blunder and turned it into a practical joke.

"I had never seen red champagne in my life, and there was a big crystal bowl of caviar. I was very happy. There was a general on each side and I offered them some of my special treat, but they refused, and I ate too much. For a number of years after that I could not face caviar even in small portions.

"The Embassy was surrounded by a big park, and we had to tighten security almost to the point of having a seemingly nonchalant man behind every tree. The people who were serving felt great anxiety, but everyone was excited about being a part of the history-making conference. It gave us a sense of great satisfaction to see the world leaders getting together right in the heat of the war and trying to reach an understanding. There was a feeling of assurance that we would work together and win a victory over the common enemy.

"Churchill presented a sword to Stalin in the name of King George VI in appreciation for the courage and valor of the defenders of Stalingrad. I was standing nearby and was very proud to be present at the ceremony. Now the sword is displayed at the Central Museum in Volgograd.

"We, in intelligence, were not to talk about our work. Many members of my family never knew that I was in Tehran. My father and step-father knew I was working at the conference but we never exchanged words about it. When you took an assignment it was understood that no one would ask questions, and they never did. There were too many members of my family who were working in intelligence, and it was a family tradition that nothing about any work we were doing would be discussed.

"I don't understand people with loose tongues. We were told that once you enter into intelligence service, you do what you do, you are finished, you close the door, you forget about it, and you don't speak about it ever. To this day some of my friends do not know that I worked at the Tehran Conference. It was not until the fiftieth anniversary of the end of World War II was celebrated that my participation in the conference became known. Now many articles are being written and videos are being made.

"When the conference was over I was preparing to return to Moscow. The intelligence officer in the Soviet Embassy decided to have me stay longer because there were American troops in Iran with Lend-Lease, and they wanted to visit the site of the conference. Since I had been the hostess for their president, I was to remain for several months and take the GIs on tour of the site. They asked questions and took pictures and showed great interest in what had happened in the Soviet Embassy. Telling the story over and over again was a very pleasant duty for me.

"They were surprised to hear that President Roosevelt had stayed in the Soviet Embassy—in the mansion. I showed them the autographed picture the President had given me. In 1951 when my step-father, Eitingon, was arrested, this picture, along with a large stack of conference pictures, was confiscated and never returned.

"I told the GIs that Stalin stayed in another house at the Embassy, and Churchill lived in the British Embassy across the street. Molotov and Voroshilov stayed in another house in the Embassy Park. I had no idea where members of the delegation or the security lived. I had an apartment in the city, but during the conference I had no time to go to the city because I had to stay in the vicinity of the Embassy in case I was needed at any time since they were adding duties which were previously not thought of. I had a folding cot in the mansion basement where the big samovar nearly exploded.

"Shortly after the conference, General McConnelly gave a dinner for the Soviet officers, and I was invited as the only woman.

This was my first experience with protocol. I realized how unprepared I was for such functions. Most of the guests were American officers with a few Soviets sitting around. An American officer came to me and said, 'You know, you have become a pin-up girl!' I had no idea what a pin-up girl was at the time so I asked him to explain it to me. He said, 'A pin-up girl is a girl who is very famous, fans put your picture on their walls.' I found out later that he was the officer who was responsible for clearing all the letters written by the GIs to their friends and families. He knew what they were writing and saw the pictures they were sending home. After I took them on the tours of the conference scene I seemed to be ever present in their letters. They did not realize they were writing history in their personal notes.

"I was talking to the American officer and wondering when we would be invited to the dinner table. Then one of the General's aides named Mitchell, came up to me and said in Russian, 'Are you going to keep us from the table much longer?' Me? What do you mean? Then he explained that as the only lady present I should be escorted to the table. I blushed because I didn't know how to go about doing things socially, but I followed and when we got to the table I was sitting to the right of the General as his guest of honor.

"A large carafe of wine was being passed around, but these were traditions with which I was not familiar. It was the first time I had been present at a dinner where the waiter came and stood with his tray until the guests helped themselves. I felt very uncomfortable. Finally, they served french fries, my favorite food. After that they served chicken, and when I cut into it the knife slipped, and the french fries flipped from the plate onto the table! I made a vow, 'Lady, you have got to learn the ABCs of table manners!' Now, for years I have been teaching delegations who go abroad, especially those going for the first time. I also taught the wives of the young diplomats about protocol and table manners and how to plan and host receptions.

"I remember the whole experience in Tehran as a wonderful time in my life. We all felt that we had gotten closer and would be able to work out our problems. After the conference, I wrote a lengthy memorandum detailing my functions, and the errors that occurred because this was the first international conference in which the Soviets had participated. There were no precedents for planning the details, and there were so many things that I did not know. Later at Yalta and Potsdam we were better organized at the service level because we had learned so much in the challenging conference in Tehran.

"When the Cold War came later, many of us simply could not understand how it could happen. Knowing so many of the U.S. and British personnel during the war, it was impossible to think of [them] as enemies. We had been comrades in arms, and I really couldn't comprehend what brought on this sudden change."

When Zoya returned to Moscow, she requested of KGB Intelligence that she be enrolled in the Language Military School to continue working and attending classes in French. Permission was granted.

She really wanted to learn Spanish because her step-father was assigned to Spain during the Civil War in 1936-37, and he had many records of Spanish songs and music. Spanish Communists often came to their home during those years, and afterward Zoya fell in love with their language. She loved the people. And when the first Spanish orphans were sent to Odessa the family did all they could to help them. The Soviets took the children into Pioneer Camps and taught them Russian. "I remember being invited to the wedding of a Soviet Pioneer leader who was the first Soviet to fall in love with a Spanish girl. It was a special occasion for us because it was the first time we had witnessed Communist solidarity, and this was before World War II.

"It so happened that when I was released from Iran, the courses in the Language Military School had already started. As an exception they accepted me, but enrolled me in French because I had studied the language in Turkey and had a foundation. I couldn't start Spanish because the class had started sometime before and the students had already learned the basics.

"When I went to Iran I had only two years of university education and was very anxious to complete a degree. My stay in Iran was from October 1943 to April 1944, so when I got back to Moscow it was an awkward time to enroll anywhere but in the Language Military School.

"At the school we were taught basic French by lovely, older ladies, some of whom were countesses before 1917. They had spoken French since childhood, but had never taught the language they knew so well. They knew nothing about methods. They taught by intuition. They were dear, elderly people, and many of the things they taught me stood me in good stead long afterward when I began teaching languages.

"They also taught us manners and etiquette. They would not speak Russian to us at all. We had to listen to French radio, but it was so rapid we had a hard time. We persisted and in a couple of months we could reproduce the information directly into French. Those elderly ladies worked miracles with us as young students.

"I never knew their life story. They were apolitical and were given a free hand in choosing teaching materials. The KGB school considered them excellent teachers and good role models.

"Because I had learned some French in Turkey, and the older ladies were so fluent and could share their expertise, my studies at the Language Military School were shortened. I got my diploma in 1945 and at the same time, after six years of candidacy, I was reinstated into the Communist Party. The Secretary of the Party Bureau, Mr. Antonov, knew me from my years in Komsomol, and he gave me the needed reference. Otherwise having a probation of six years would have been difficult to explain. So 1945 was an eventful year for me."

CHAPTER 2

Yalta, Potsdam, Nuremberg, and the Atomic Bomb Papers

THE YALTA CONFERENCE was set for February 1945 to be held near Yalta in Crimea, USSR. The leaders were British Prime Minister Churchill, U.S. President F. D. Roosevelt, and Soviet Premier Stalin, representing the major allied powers in World War II. Some of the chief decisions agreed upon by the "Big Three" were: (1) a four power occupation of Germany with France being the fourth power; (2) a founding conference for the UN to be held later that year; (3) the Soviet Union's agreement to enter the war against Japan after Germany's defeat, receiving occupation areas in the East in return; and (4) a guarantee of representative government in Poland. These agreements were so secret and complex that they were considered by some to be undue concessions to the Soviet Union. The Yalta Conference has long been the subject of heated controversy.

Zoya was sent to Yalta as a liaison officer between the three delegations. There the delegation residences were very far apart. The Livadyisky Palace was the residence of President Roosevelt and his staff. This was where the official sessions took place. A former summer residence of the Russian Czars, it was converted to a sanitarium for Trade Union members after the Bolshevik Revolution. In 1980 it was made into a museum dedicated to the Yalta Conference.

The residence of Stalin was on a hill in the former Yusupovsky Palace. Before the revolution this palace belonged to Count Yusupov who master-minded and took part in the assassination of Rasputin. Much further out on the coast road was the residence of Winston Churchill in the Vorontsovsky Palace which was built by Count Vorontsov who had once been the Russian Ambassador to Great Britain. Therefore the architecture and interior resembled British castles.

"I helped with arrangements in the residence of Prime Minister Churchill before his arrival. From the outset, he was not happy with Yalta as the location for this conference. Apparently he did not like the palace, but as days went by the weather was very good, and he began to enjoy the palace and the wonderful winter garden.

"President Roosevelt suggested six different locations for the conference, but Stalin insisted on Yalta. The President was so intent on having the conference as soon as possible he agreed with Stalin's chosen location. I didn't know very much about high level political conferences at Tehran, but by the time of Yalta I had learned a lot. I understood more about what was happening and how it related to the deliberation. Later I came to understand how important the Yalta Conference was by reading different documents and memoirs of contemporary political figures and historians. I believe that this conference was decisive for the last stage of the war. Through the prism of the celebration of fifty years of victory in 1995, I would say that it was pivotal for Stalin's official agreement to enter the war in the Far East and his statement that it would happen after the victory in Europe. He kept his commitment.

"The Soviets started their offensive against Japan on August 8, 1945, and we had ended the war in Europe on the eighth of May. As Stalin had promised, when unconditional surrender was signed in Karlshof near Berlin, in just exactly three months his troops were in place and ready to help defeat Japan. Documents pertaining to the Yalta Conference were published, and I translated a number of them which gave me an opportunity to study and analyze them. While working in Yalta I observed the delegations and had a lot to do with the content of the discussion from the Soviet side at the time. Now, fifty years later, the results of the Yalta Conference are still being debated.

"Each side had its own evaluation of the decisions. There was a wide belief that President Roosevelt was not in physical condition to make major decisions, and that was the reason that he gave in to Stalin. I think this was not quite true—Stalin was a very shrewd negotiator. He knew what he wanted, and he did not go back on his commitment to the allies. He was eager to prove that once he made a commitment he would honor it. Our people had already gone through the worst of the tragedies of the war by February. He knew that the war was coming to an end and we knew that the Allied troops in Europe were some five hundred kilometers from Berlin and the Soviet Troops were approximately fifty kilometers away.

"It was a controversial subject, and the Allied Troops were not too happy to push on because they knew there would be many casualties. The Soviet troops had suffered severely and they were prepared for any casualties to achieve victory. They wanted to end the war in Berlin just as they had wanted to end the Patriotic War in 1812 in Paris."

When Stalin agreed to enter the war with Japan, he made certain demands, and they were agreed to by both Roosevelt and Churchill. In return for the Soviet commitment, the Russians were to get the city of Dairen as a seaport on the East coast, four islands in the Kuriles, and half of Sakhalin. It was agreed that after victory over Japan, the Soviet Union would receive the port and islands in return for their military contributions.

On the 6th of August, two days before the Soviets entered the war with Japan, the atomic bomb was dropped on Hiroshima. Stalin took it as a betrayal and believed that it was done to intimidate the Soviets. He saw it as a way to show the Russians that they were not that strong. Many Soviets joined Stalin in the belief that the Allies didn't need them anymore. They all wondered if it would have been the same had President Roosevelt lived.

Truman was quite a different personality. "I don't mean that we would have been embracing each other with friendship after the war but we certainly would not have become enemies. Truman's anti-

Communist, anti-Soviet attitude changed relations drastically. This was the beginning of the Cold War.

"When Mr. Dulles became secretary of state in the United States, and the time came to work out the wording of the peace treaty with Japan, everybody seemed to have forgotten about the earlier agreement with Stalin in Yalta. It wasn't mentioned in any of the papers. So Japan said, 'We don't know anything about the agreement. We were not a part of the international meeting.' Indeed, it was a confidential agreement. After so many years have passed we need to open up the archives and find out what the confidential agreement really says.

"I don't think the Japanese will just give up those islands to the Russians, but it would seem to be time for the American and British leaders to become mediators between the Russians and the Japanese on this simmering issue. To my mind that would be the best solution because it is still a deadlock.

"I am trying, in this book, to avoid evaluation of the leading political characters because I am speaking as a person who served my country. I was not directly involved in policy making, but I knew it all through translation and being an interpreter. I was honored to be present and to be a witness to so much. I had my own evaluation and assessment of what was going on and even though we held on to the port of Dairen, we returned it to the Chinese People's Republic when we became friendly with them. The time will probably come when the islands will be returned to Japan.

"Soviet—Russian people have lived on the Sakhalin Islands for fifty years just as they have in other republics in the Soviet Union. In Russia we have many problems to face with whole blocks of nationalities and ethnic groups (including Chechnya) which were uprooted at the end of World War II by Stalin and forcefully deported to the Republics of Central Asia being accused of treason during the German occupation. At the time of *Perestroika* they were all acquitted, but no measures were taken by the government to reinstate them properly. Their lands were inhabited all these years by different people. The issue still persists, and this is the reason that the people living on the Kurile Islands are adamant about remaining in their homes. After fifty years they have nothing in their former homeland to go back to. It has been made a political issue instead of trying to settle the problem. Chechnya is the perfect example.

All of this confusion and misery came out of the confidential decisions made at Yalta more than fifty years ago.

"Soon after I returned from Yalta, I was assigned to the 'S' Department in the KGB under Sudoplatov. This department was dealing with the Atomic Bomb Papers. I was summoned to his office and was told that for a period of time I would be the one dealing with important secret papers which I had to translate. There were photocopies of documents which were very technical. Other translators would be screened and brought into this 'S' Department to translate some of the papers, but that would take time, and the papers needed to be deciphered quickly. They trusted me because they said I could carry on the work of my father, Vasily Zarubin. He was head of Soviet Foreign Intelligence in the United States during World War II. They told me that I would be translating these very important papers which he had been instrumental in getting for the Soviets.

"I learned later that there was much discussion about Academician Kurchatov. Much is being written about him now—what he knew about the papers from translations, but at times shared the information with colleagues as his own ideas. It was even rumored that he hid the possession of the U.S. atomic bomb blueprint from his colleagues.

"I didn't know any of this was going on because I was closed up in a separate room. A big safe was moved in where I could keep all the papers and translations. I was given a dictionary, and as I started looking at it, there was not a word about the scientific terms I needed. One word really gave me trouble, and that was the word 'pile'. That was a coded term, and it took some time of struggling to crack it. I knew many of the words separately, but when I put them together, they made no sense. I had a technical dictionary which was little help. My boss finally came in and said that I would have an appointment with Academician Kurchatov who headed the technical side of the Soviet atomic project.

"When I read some of what I translated to him, he said, 'My dear girl, when did you graduate from school?' I told him 1939 and he responded, 'you have forgotten your physics! What you have done is absolute nonsense. Go back and work on it again and read your physics!'

"I was close to tears because the wording in the papers was not language to me—it was gobbledygook. But little by little I learned. I met with Kurchatov several times and had gotten into the physics a bit deeper. One day he listened to what I had translated and said, 'Hey! Now there is some light in it. Come on and read it again.' Later when I saw *My Fair Lady* and Professor Higgins, I remembered how Mr. Kurchatov made me feel.

"By this time we had more technical translators coming in. Some of them were brought from the Urals and some from Central Asia. I believe some of them were brought from prison, but that was just my impression since no one talked about it, but their haunted look suggested suffering. I was one of the coordinators on the linguistic side, not the technical side.

"I did get a personal assignment to translate a confidential report titled *Atomic Energy* by Smith. Many of the scientists believed that the report was the essence or idea of the power of atomic energy—that it was not the theory. They believed that it was a report on the research in the field. It makes me wonder what Mr. Sudoplatov meant when he wrote about Robert Oppenheimer in his book, *Special Tasks,* because I am sure this is not the way it was. I know for sure that those papers were sent to us by supporters of the Soviet Union who wanted us to succeed in destroying fascism and wanted us to share the secrets of the ultimate weapon with the Americans and British. This sentiment was very much echoed by the memorandum of Bertrand Russell and Albert Einstein when they addressed the United States president and the whole world saying that atomic energy should not be released without international control.

"I worked very diligently with the translation of the papers. It was a tedious job for me because I was more of a speaking interpreter, but I was honored to be chosen for the job. I knew the English language and could express myself well, but just sitting with technical papers and not being a scientist was very difficult.

"When I read . . . *Special Tasks,* written by the Schecters of Washington, D.C., I was angered by his implying that my father had gotten the papers. It was as if he had said to me, 'your father has stolen these papers, from Oppenheimer, you come on and translate them.' That is not true. When I was given the assignment to translate the papers this is what was said to me, 'You must translate these documents because it is a family affair. Your father contributed to it.' I understood that my step-mother, Liza, was involved because they worked together. My father never asked me what I translated. Nor did I ask him if he got those papers."

The Potsdam Conference in Germany was set for July 1945. It was a summit meeting between Stalin, Truman, Churchill, and (later on) Clement Attlee. The change of leadership in the United States, after Roosevelt's death, made a difference. Truman's attitude toward the Communists made it difficult to reach an agreement on the wide range of problems which had to be settled concerning Germany. The conference issued an ultimatum to Japan. Almost all of the agreements accepted during the conference were breached as the Cold War became more intense.

Zoya went to Potsdam to serve as the liaison between the delegations. She helped the Soviet staff communicate with the British and Americans. While Truman and Churchill were evasively trying to tell Stalin about the atomic bomb, he was nonchalant and indifferent because he already knew about it. The translation on the papers was a confining job, and now that more translators were available, she felt the need for change. She had been working on the translation of the Atomic Bomb Papers since March of 1945. Six months was a long time to be closed up in a room with information not exciting to her.

"I continued to do whatever I was assigned to do in Department 'S,' but I finally decided that it was time to continue my studies. After some anxious times I finally got permission by going to a very high level authority. They took into consideration the services I was rendering to the country, even though they did not readily let intelligence officers leave to study. They permitted me to enroll in Moscow University, but when they told me I would have to stay 3½ or 4 years to get my certificate [degree], I knew I couldn't do that. A friend suggested that I go to the Institute of Foreign Languages. I did not want to become a professor of languages, but I did want my university certificate.

"I went to the institute as a war veteran in uniform, and said I would like to enter for those who had been in the war. War veterans had special privileges for entering universities. There were no competitive examinations. We took oral tests in English, and I was enrolled as a third year student. That was in 1945, but I was so busy with work I had to wait until 1947 to start my studies. I took examinations every other week and some by correspondence. I also became interested in teaching methods. I graduated in 1949. Later on the teaching methods came to my rescue. When I was dismissed from the KGB in 1951 after my step-father was sent to prison, I became a teacher. Many of my colleagues who were my teachers as I was finishing university work told me that they were intimidated when I wanted to come into their classes because they would have to be on guard about their manner of speaking. 'You spoke such beautiful English as compared to our language, and we didn't want you to know that we were not so good in oral speech.'

"They were great enthusiasts, but I visited their classes because I needed to get my apprenticeship in teaching, and I wanted to learn teaching methods. I loved their devotion to the language, and their love for teaching. They spoke English with a Russian accent, and they mispronounced words but that was not important to me. I was getting what I had to have for that university certificate.

"All the time I was studying I continued working for foreign intelligence, but after I graduated in 1949, I got special permission from the KGB to teach at night, working on a per hour basis to get experience. I went to the Institute two evenings a week and continued to do so for two academic years until October 1951."

The Nuremberg Trials were conducted by the United States, the Soviet Union, Great Britain, and France from November 1945 through October 1946. During this time Zoya continued her work with Intelligence and her studies. She was also on call as a liaison between the representatives of the four countries in Nuremberg for three-and-a-half months. Then Sudaplatov called her back to Moscow to continue translating the atomic bomb papers. The accused Germans (who included von Ribbentrop, Goering, Hess, and the heads of the German armed forces) were tried for three kinds of crimes: Crimes Against Peace (planning and waging aggressive war); War Crimes (murder or mistreatment of civilians or prisoners of war, killing of hostages, and plunder of property or wanton destruction of communities); Crimes Against Humanity (extermination or enslavement of any civilian population before or during the war on political, racial, or religious grounds). The trials established new principles in the law of nations, the highest of which was that every person is responsible for his or her own acts.

CHAPTER 3

The Early Years

ZOYA ZARUBINA WAS BORN in Perovo (now one of the boroughs of Moscow), April 5, 1920, into a society where philosophically everyone was equal. Soviets conformed to the rules of the Party as established by Lenin and secured by Stalin. The Bolsheviks had carried on a revolution until they brought down the Czar in 1917. Her father had been involved in the revolution and joined the Communist Party in 1918. Zoya's birth came right in the midst of the Civil War.

When she was two-and-a-half years of age, her father was sent to the Far East to establish Soviet power. She and her mother went to join him in Vladivostok on the Pacific coast. They were in Vladivostok for a short while when her father received an assignment to go to Harbin in China to take part in the repatriation of the White Russians who fled from the country during the Civil War and wanted to return. Harbin was at the end of the railroad line going out of Russia. This circumstance had created a large settlement of White Russians. Vasily Zarubin's duty, in part, was to help them fill out the necessary papers for repatriation. They stayed in Harbin until the end of 1925, when her father was summoned to return to Moscow for a new assignment. He was needed for work in Europe.

Zoya's mother was getting the official papers in order to follow her husband back to Moscow, but a letter came from an anonymous "well-wisher" reporting that Zarubin was being unfaithful to her. She completed the papers and waited for approval.

While her mother was working, as all good Soviets did, things were not organized for child care so Zoya played around in the lobby of the hotel. Zoya says, "I knew the hotel inside out and many of the comrades had worked with my father, Zarubin. Uncle Zyama was always friendly and would pat me on the back and greet me. One day he came up to me and said, 'I want you to meet Uncle Leonid. He has just arrived and he will live here too!' Later I was with my mother in the lobby and introduced her to Uncle Leonid. It was love at first sight, and she loved him for the rest of her life, even when he was unfaithful to her." When Leonid Eitingon, who was the new Vice Consul in Harbin, suggested to her mother that they join him at his next assignment in Peking, her mother accepted, and he tore up her official papers for the return to Moscow. She was vulnerable because of the letter she had received about her husband's infidelity.

Leonid Eitingon had a special assignment in Peking where they lived in the settlement next to the Embassy. There was no Soviet school, and the Russian language was not taught. So Zoya went to an American school.

The Soviet Union was just beginning, but forceful things were happening. Zoya loved her new step-father, and he recognized that even at a very early age she was bright and loved adventure.

When they arrived in Peking, Leonid left them in the hotel and went to the Embassy. Her mother told her that they needed food because they were hungry. She had tried through sign language and a dictionary she had to communicate with the hotel employees that they wanted food. The Chinese men smiled and nodded as if they understood, but instead of food they brought her a folding cot for Zoya. She tells the story of her first challenge to learn another language, "My mother started crying, and we didn't get anything to eat until Leonid returned from the Embassy. I was learning English in the American school, but I loved my mother very much, and it hurt me to see her cry so I learned Chinese, too. I spoke Russian at home all of the time, English my first year in school, and learned enough Chinese to help my mother. My knowledge of Chinese was very helpful after my half-sister was born prematurely October 30, 1927, and we had to have a Chinese *amah.*"

Zoya was active and inquisitive. She loved to ride her bicycle. Everyone in the settlement teased her and said if she could go to bed with the bicycle, she would do it. The moment she got up in the morning she started doing all sorts of errands for her mother and Leonid in the vast territory of the Embassy compound.

She made a bet with someone relating to the wall which divided the Soviet and American Embassies. On one side of the wall there was Soviet territory, and on the other side there was American territory. "I made the bet that I could ride the bike on top of that wall, and I did, but when I got almost to the end I waved my hand in the air, lost my balance, and fell into the American territory!" The Americans brought her back to her compound. She hoped nobody would know, and the incident would be forgotten.

The next day there was a Soviet dinner party in a big hall with beautiful mahogany tables and chairs. When Zoya walked into the room, one of the men said in a very firm voice, "You know there was a story in the paper this morning about a big disturbance in the diplomatic circles. It seems that we broke the borders of the American territory." Zoya remembers, "I sat there stunned and afraid. I really didn't know that they were just teasing me." Then the man continued, "A certain person crossed the border."

"Now I realized that everyone knew about it so I told the whole story—about the bet and how I had won."

Always forward and thinking ahead, even as a young child, Zoya's precociousness appealed to Leonid. He took her with him on several train trips. While they were traveling he would always give her his watch and say, "Zoya, the minute this hand reaches this place, wake me up."

"It became a game. I kept the watch and was careful to keep up with what he had asked me to do because I was away from the routine at the Embassy, and that was fun. One time we were traveling on one of his business trips, and someone knocked at the door loudly. Leonid gave me a doll to hold before he opened the door. I had never liked dolls, but I held on to it while they searched the compartment and tore it apart. They didn't find anything and walked out. Leonid closed the door quickly, took the doll, and I saw him take something out of the doll—a piece of paper—and started chewing it up. I said, 'What are you doing?' And he put his finger to his lips for silence. Then he said, 'Don't tell anyone!' It became a game, and I followed it very diligently."

Later there was another episode aboard ship on the Yellow Sea. "I loved to go to the sea because I was a strong swimmer and was not afraid of strange waters. We were somewhere out on the Yellow Sea, and Leonid was sleeping in the cabin when some Chinese men came up to me on deck and started asking questions about my step-father. They told me that he was a bad man, and they were going to do something about it. By then I knew enough Chinese to under-stand what they were saying. Then they began asking me questions and wanted me to tell them about Leonid. I screamed, 'Leave me alone, leave me alone!' and ran into the restroom. I was afraid of the Chinese men because of the things they were saying about my step-father and me. Then they took the handle off the restroom door so I couldn't get out.

"I knew Leonid was asleep so I opened the porthole and shouted, 'Uncle Leonid, I am stuck in the toilet and I am jumping out into the water!' One of my feet was already out when he came and dragged me out of that porthole and brought me back into the cabin. He closed the door and held onto me and said, 'I was so frightened. I was sleeping when all of a sudden I heard your voice from the sea (he heard it from the porthole), and you were saying that someone locked you in the restroom.'

"Uncle Leonid and I were very good friends, and I idolized him in the sense that he was a handsome man, and he was strong and big and very kind to me. We were a good team, and I traveled with him often and did whatever he needed to have me do.

"After my sister Svetlana was born, I began to feel neglected. Of course, the attention was divided, and I was no longer the center of adult attention so I decided to make them think I had run away. I was seven years old at the time, and I thought the best way to disappear was to hide in the wardrobe. I sat there for hours and nobody was looking for me so I decided it wasn't worthwhile. I loved my sister very dearly, but I was not ready to give up all the special attention."

Svetlana was born prematurely in 1927 because of the turmoil created when Chiang Kai-shek's troops occupied the Soviet settlement where the family lived. There was a very narrow pathway between the settlement and the Embassy compound. The troops could not come into the Embassy compound so they created havoc in the settlement.

"My mother was pregnant and very disturbed because the troops directed all of us into the dining room in a very rough way while at the same time throwing things around and rounding up and arresting Russian students who were practitioners in the Institute of Oriental Studies in Moscow. They were in Peking as students learning the Chinese language. There were about ten of them.

"The residents of the settlement knew that I was a venturing and aggressive child so the women asked me to run to first one apartment and then another to find out what had happened in their apartments while the troops were there. Mother told me not to go to our apartment so I went to the club house and found that Lenin's portrait had been torn down, benches turned over, and there was a lot of water in the room. I don't remember seeing other children, but by evening some of the soldiers left and some stayed to keep the women surrounded.

"I went to the gate of the Embassy so I could speak to the diplomats, and Leonid was standing nearby. He asked me what was happening, and I gave him the details. He leaned over and whispered to me to go to our apartment and look for something in a drawer that was wrapped up and bring it to him. I went straight to our apartment and was angry and heartbroken because I saw all of my seventh birthday toys which I had received just the day before, broken and scattered all over the room.

"I found the wrapped package in the drawer. Of course, I looked inside, and it was a revolver. Even as a child my first thought was that he must be on some kind of secret mission, and I was a part of the game. I was happy that I could help him so I took it straight back to the Embassy fence.

"Two or three hours later when it was very dark, all of us in the settlement were brought into the territory of the Soviet Embassy. We were brought into a big hall where mattresses had been placed, and people could sleep after the harrowing day.

"Mother and I didn't stay there, and I don't know why, but probably because Leonid was a high ranking officer. He left us in the residence of the consulate with the admonition that we were to stay there and not move. His instructions were definite that we were to stay put until he returned. I was trying to be obedient, but there was a big watch dog, and he was taking his job very seriously. I needed to urinate desperately, and the dog would not let me move. There was a potted palm tree near me, and I finally urinated on the palm. When Leonid returned he asked if everything were all right, and I burst into tears. He tried to console me, and when I told him about the dog and the palm tree, they all had a good laugh. I was a tomboy so escapades of any kind were really fun.

"Leonid came to me one day and told me that something had happened to my mother. She had become very ill and was in an American hospital. Then he told me that I had a baby sister—a very tiny one. A Cesarean section had been performed at six months. Leonid took me to the hospital and when we got to the room there was a cradle right in the middle of the room. No one was there, just something covered in the cradle. I came up close and peeked in, but didn't see anything. Then they unfolded the cotton blanket and there was a tiny creature like a little bird. She weighed just a kilo and a half [3.3 pounds]. My first thought was what kind of a sister is that?

"We had to have an *amah*—a Chinese woman who fed the baby because Mother didn't have any milk. So I became the negotiator for Mother because by this time I understood and spoke Chinese very well. All the things the *amah* wanted to tell Mother and vice versa would be interpreted by me. We followed the same procedure with the cook. I don't know why, but when we sat down to dinner there would always be about twelve people so Mother would tell me how much food we needed to buy and what to cook, and I would tell the cook in Chinese.

"When I went to school a rickshaw would come and pick me up. One day I decided that I wanted to pull the rickshaw. I tried and couldn't get it going, but at the dinner table that night there was conversation about me again. One person said, 'We have a scandal on our hands. The foreigners are taking the jobs away from the rickshaw drivers!' I always seemed to be the brunt of their joking conversation, but it did not stop my venturing spirit.

"Leonid involved me in so many of his business trips, I became accustomed to his special attention. My mother would scold him saying, 'What is the matter with you? You have this lovely baby girl—your own daughter. Why do you pay so little attention to her and so much attention to Zoya?' He would always answer with, 'Zoya is such a clever little girl and this one is still too little.' She did not know that he was letting me do special things for him.

"He was always very kind to me. You would never have known that I was not his daughter. Once I asked him if I could call him 'father.' He said, 'No, you have a father who is a very distinguished man whom I respect. You just call me Uncle Leonid.' And I called him that for the rest of his life."

Zoya finally assumed the role of an older sister. On one occasion she was left alone with the baby. Her mother told her that the doctor would come, and she gave her the questions to ask him in English. She had to think carefully because her classes at school were in English. She spoke Russian at home, but not being able to write the language, she had to retain instructions and translate them from memory. Her mother had not returned when the doctor came so Zoya followed her instructions and got all of the information her mother wanted. Then she told the doctor she had another very important request. "You see she is my sister and her ears stick out— I don't like that! What can we do about it?" The doctor told her it was very easy. Just go to the pharmacy and get some plaster and plaster her ears flat to her head. "I was so enthusiastic; I ordered the car and went to get the prescriptions and the plaster. By the time mother got home I had the baby's ears plastered flat to her head. Mother was horrified. Then I told her that I had plastered her ears like that because it was the recommendation of the doctor. Mother was so upset about it, I finally had to confess that I had complained to the doctor about her ears sticking out, and he suggested the plasters."

When her sister was a year old they had a big party and let the *amah* bring the child into the room. Zoya says, "We were all flabbergasted when she came in with little Svetlana dressed in a Chinese hat and kimono, and the *amah* had made special slippers for her that looked like little piglets. This was the *amah's* gift to my sister. The *amah* was very proud of her work, and Mother did not want to offend her, though it was a shock to see the little white face peering out from all the Chinese regalia."

The *amah* had her own four children behind the Chinese wall and would visit them periodically. "But when we left China she was running after the train crying because she knew it was the last time she would see her Russian baby."

China was an interesting and exciting time in Zoya's life, and much of it she remembers in detail—almost as if she had been in training for intelligence work since early childhood. It was in China that she met Rudolph Abel. "Fifty years later when I saw a magazine article about his being arrested in America, my reaction was that it couldn't be Rudolph Abel because he used to play tennis with me when I was a child in China. He didn't have any children of his own, and he was a very nice man who liked children. He was a radio operator in China at that time. Recently his picture was in the Soviet press. Now that all of the archives are open we get new information. He was from Latvia. Later Willy Fisher took his name as a legendary cover-up when he went to America for undercover work after Rudolph Abel had died."

Leonid was briefly called back to Moscow. The grandmother in Perovo, where Zoya was born, was excited about having a new grandchild. She would be taking care of her while her mother worked, but there was a problem. Svetlana's baby talk was very Chinese. Once again Zoya became the interpreter.

While the family was in Moscow they lived at the Metropole Hotel. Zoya's playground was Red Square and Saint Basil's Cathedral. The Metropole was close to Leonid's work, and they had no home in Moscow so it was logical during the interim to live at the hotel.

Each morning after breakfast, Zoya would go to Red Square and climb on the Kremlin Wall. She had a good time at St. Basil's because there were so many interesting things to see.

The family often visited with Zoya's *babushka* (grandmother) in Perovo. Her mother had one brother and two sisters and they were a close-knit family. The house in Perovo was a log house that the family found many years ago to use as a *dacha*, or vacation house, for the summer. But when World War I came, they got stuck there, and it became permanent for Zoya's grandmother and her children. In the early days it took about thirty minutes by electric train to get from Perovo to the center of Moscow.

The stay in Moscow was short because Leonid was reassigned to Turkey. When the family arrived, Zoya was enrolled in an English high school for girls. The year was 1929, and they would stay in Turkey for two years—long enough for Zoya to add some of the native language and French to her linguistic accumulation. Her schoolmates made fun of her because she spoke with an American accent so she had to adapt to the British accent. She was closer to the Turkish girls who were from wealthy families. It was an expensive school. One of the teachers asked her if she would like to come to a special class on Saturdays on scriptures. She replied that she would have to find out from her parents if they wanted her to be in the scripture class. "I went home and told my mother that they were going to teach violin lessons at school, and that I would like to go to the class on Saturdays. The word for violin in Russian is *scripka*. Mother said that they didn't mind because it was not far from the Embassy. So they would be glad to have me go to the special lessons.

"I went to the scripture class the next Saturday, and it had nothing to do with the violin. I had to walk out of the class and go home to tell Mother that they were not talking about the violin, they were talking about God. That was the end of the Saturday lessons."

She took French as an added language in the Turkish English Language School, and by the age of ten she could communicate in Russian, English, Chinese, Turkish, and French. Her big disadvantage continued to be that she had not learned to write her own native language.

Later she definitely learned that Leonid's assignment in Turkey was to catch up with Trotsky, the brilliant Jew who was in competition with Stalin for leadership of the country after the death of Lenin. "I am sure he had other assignments but the important things do not appear in . . . *Special Tasks* which presumes to know so much about my family and does not always give correct information.

"Trotsky lived on a little island called Prinkipo in Turkey. There was a large number of White Russian immigrants in Turkey who had fled from the Bolshevik Revolution in 1922. When my parents went to work I would look into the desk drawer and found interesting books which told about the White Russian immigrants. My parents were quite surprised when I talked about the White Russian immigrants, and I never told them that I had found the books in the desk drawer.

"One day we read in the papers that there was a fire on the Island of Prinkipo where Trotsky lived. It reported that Trotsky was saved without being harmed. He left the country, and very shortly after that Eitingon took us back to Moscow, and he was later reassigned to Spain as deputy resident for Soviet intelligence. During the civil war he recruited a number of Spanish Communists to fight against Trotsky's followers. When the civil war ended, Eitingon returned to Moscow, and much later was given the assignment by Stalin to eliminate Trotsky.

"When I started school in Moscow I came home one day and told Mother that everyone was calling me an American. 'They are calling me names and I do not want to wear these stupid clothes. I want to be like everybody else.' "

That attitude stuck with her because when we were shopping in 1993 in Austin, Texas, she would look at stylish suits and dresses which she really liked but thought a bit dressy. She would pass them by, saying, "I can't wear this back in Moscow. It is important not to dress better than your friends. I learned early in life in my country it is detrimental to stand out. Not that I am afraid of it—I just don't want to. I feel so much for my people, and it hurts me that there is so much in our experience that I cannot explain to everybody. Much of my life was more privileged, but I wouldn't say that I have the right to wear what I want to wear, or that I really deserve it. I see how other people are judged, and I don't want that to happen to me. I want my people to judge me by what I am, not how I am dressed."

The return from Turkey to Moscow placed Zoya in a new world. The family lived in the first cooperative house designed for military and intelligence officers. It was a building with a special history because many of the residents were arrested and eliminated or threw themselves out of upper story windows during arrests. It was the period of Stalinist purges.

The KGB set up a special school—No. 50—for the many children whose families were connected with Intelligence. It was an experimental school with the best qualified teachers for the higher grades. Many of them were university professors who, when they were told to come teach in the experimental school sponsored by the KGB, could not refuse. The school was a distance from the building where they lived so the children had to arrange their own transportation which was unusual in the Soviet Union. Most children attended the school nearest their homes.

The children in the experimental school received an excellent education, and the teachers were outstanding role models for them. This was definitely education with a purpose. Not all of the students were children of intelligence officers. Some of them were the children of the support staff.

It was in the experimental school that Zoya became active in many fields, particularly sports. She was one of the initiators of the first Soviet Youth Sports Club. Because it was under the supervision of the KGB it was called the Youth Dynamo Club, and was added to the existing Dynamo Club for Adults. Zoya spent a lot of time with track and field, basketball, and volleyball. The stadium was far, and the students had to go by tram. It was difficult to get regular meals.

"My mother would often say to me: 'What do you think you are doing? You are wasting your time running and jumping instead of studying music.' I had music lessons, and my mother thought I had musical talent. Her friend was a music teacher and encouraged me. But my interest was in sports, and I continued until I excelled in the field.

"I was living a privileged life and was not aware of the extreme hardships many people were facing. I was elated because I was head of everything—at the top of my class in my studies, tops in sports, and always the emcee in all the big concerts given for the students. We liked to dance and sing, but were not permitted to do Western European dances—that was considered bourgeois. We all loved to dance. Most teen-agers enjoyed it. My half-brother Vladimir [Leonid's son] insisted that I teach him the dances, and when we were at home I taught him what I had learned in Turkey. Then there was a break-through, and we were permitted to dance all forms. Vladimir and I were the center of attention because we already knew how to do the dances.

"We were happy to have the KGB Club nearby because that is where we went after school. Since our parents worked late we could stay late at the club. We were taught how to use the radio, how to become sharp shooters, and drive a car. When Hitler was raising his ugly head in Europe through Fascism, we learned parachuting.

"I met Vasily Stalin [the son of the Soviet leader] in sports activities. He was a happy-go-lucky sort of person. When we were at the skating rink, he would go to one girl after another. His father did not like his shifting habits with women so he ordered that he settle on one girl, marry her, and go to aviation school. So he became a pilot.

"Vasily was short, red headed, and a fragile type—not handsome, but he was Stalin's son, and he wanted to make good and prove that he could really do something. He was in sports, but he wasn't much of a sportsman. He had a car, and none of the rest of us did. We were serious about sports. I learned to ride horseback and some nursing skills during this period. I also learned how to survive a chemical attack by putting on a gas mask and learned how to administer first aid to poison victims. I learned to run and jump as if in combat. I was always first to volunteer. I react quickly and get myself into many things which, on second thought, I should probably not have gotten into. But I enjoyed it all as a teen-ager. Sports became a big part of my life, and I loved the people who came to the stadium. I had a lot of friends and boyfriends.

"When I think about Vasily Stalin, I am sad. His was a tragic story from his youth. His mother was dead. His father was cold and demanding. The generals handled him carefully because he was Stalin's son. When he became a pilot, he had one family after another and became a drunkard. When Khrushchev came into power, he put Vasily in prison in the city of Vladimir.

"After primary school Leonid made the decision that I should go to school No. 50 because I could study German, and in those classes we started corresponding with German children whose parents were Communists. It was our first contact with children in Europe, and we were excited when we received answers to our letters.

"It was while we were corresponding with German children that Georgi Dimitrov, a Bulgarian Communist, was accused of setting the Reichstag on fire. There was much coverage in the newspapers, and world protests were so strong the Germans had to set him free. He came to the Soviet Union and became chairman of the Comintern (Communist International). When he arrived I had the honor of greeting him with a bouquet of flowers, probably because we were KGB children and had been screened.

"One of the best things about the club was that it gave us an opportunity to meet historical figures. They could not say, 'No!' to the children of the establishment. We heard Civil War veterans and generals who were fighting the Japanese in Khalin Gol. Then we would have the first Soviets who were stationed at the North Pole. They were called Papanintsi after their leader, Ivan Papanin, who was a leading Arctic researcher. We also had Stakhanovtsi, a movement of workers' heroes, who always exceeded their working quotas. The five-year plans were based on the work of this group.

"In the summer we went to Pioneer summer camp and enjoyed the activity. Everything went very well, but all of a sudden we began to be aware of Stalin's victimization. This was the period when KGB officers were also being put into prison. Hearing about it was one thing, but when you knew the person involved, that was traumatic. We would come to school, and students would say: 'You know Maslennikov's father was arrested yesterday!' And then another student would tell about others. I could hardly believe it because we all thought of Stalin as a very nice man, like a grandfather. Because many of the parents had attended our sports events we knew them very well, and now they were being sent to prison.

"The building where we lived was shaped like a U turned upside down. We lived in a tall, first story apartment above the ground floor. We could hear the terrible Black Mary—a covered mini-truck used when officials came to make an arrest. It always came in the middle of the night. I heard about these things later, but I was living in the building while it was taking place. The next morning someone on the stairway would tell us that the KGB had made two arrests the night before.

"A friend of the family lived on the eighth floor. He was a very good intelligence officer. He seemed a bit elderly to me and was a little stooped. He was married to a beautiful ballerina who wore western clothes, and in those days that was very unusual. When the KGB knocked on the door in the middle of the night, he jumped from the eighth floor through a window. Later his wife became a drunkard, and this was when I realized how helpless we all were.

"Leonid would permit her to come into our home which was risky, but he was very cautious about my boyfriends. If I went out for the evening, my grandmother would always meet me at the door, and there would be a quick 'good-bye'. Leonid worked late hours, but if I brought someone in, he always wanted to know who their parents were and where they lived. He wanted to make sure that no one who could harm the family would come into our home because we could be put on the black list with the identity of our friends and associates. I did not realize until later that all of the apartments could be tapped.

"During the Pioneer camp years and then in Komsomol, I was fortunate to have really great leaders who were four or five years older. We didn't think of them as our bosses who were there to train us to be Communists or to condition us, but only as our leaders.

During this period I had many boyfriends, but they did not especially interest me. Sasha Zimin was a basketball player who was
older than I, and he would ask me to go out. I would always say I
wanted to go to the opera where there was no time for fooling
around, and we would have to go directly home when it was over.

"I met so many interesting people in my home—I was looking
more to improve my mind rather than have a special interest in
romance. I was so interested in listening to fascinating stories, my
mother would let me stay up later when she and Leonid had co-
workers as guests who told fascinating stories about their lives. I
soon learned to read between the lines, realizing that they were not
saying all that they felt or knew. Some of them had studied at the
Military Academy. Some had been dismissed. Even when I was
young I knew how much they had suffered, and I suffered with
them. I understood that their bosses didn't like them or that Stalin
had said, 'No' to them on some project. I was understanding more
through these visits, and the outside world became very challenging
to me. Leonid once said that in the 50s all you had to do to be sent
to prison was to either disagree with Stalin or be a Jew.

"My mother was working in the Gulag Department. She never
told me what she did there. I believe she was an economist. One day
something had really disturbed her at work. Leonid was not living
with us at the time. Mother took me out in the kitchen and turned
the water on in the sink. She told me I was the senior member of
the family, and she must rely on me. She showed me a drawer in the
cupboard where she had placed a bundle of warm clothes. Then she
told me that they might come and take her to prison, and she wanted me to remain calm. She told me that under the bundle of papers
there was an address of a distant relative in the country where our
babushka went to get potatoes. Then she told me that I was to take
my sister Svetlana and go there if they came for her. I was fifteen
years old and Svetlana was eight. I was learning early to be a sur-
vivor. I always did as much as I could for other people, but my primary responsibility was to my family.

"Mother continued to work and was not arrested, but we were
prepared in a turbulent time for anything that might happen. She
worked until 1941 when my daughter, Tanya, was born. Then she
stayed at home so I could volunteer as a war nurse.

"We didn't talk about serious things at home, but I always felt the tension. When Leonid was with us and had friends in, the conversation was light, and no one talked about anything current. They did a lot of smoking. Leonid didn't drink so we had a lot of tea. Seldom was there anything like a party—mostly they just played cards.

"My father, Vasily Zarubin, and his wife, Liza, were in Moscow between assignments. Both of them were intelligence officers, but my visits in their home were quite different from other intelligence families—they talked about everything. Of course, they never spoke about their assignments, but Father was fun loving and enjoyed playing the balalaika and singing so there was a very different atmosphere in his home."

When Zoya graduated from the experimental school, her father, Zarubin, was on assignment in Germany, but he wanted to be with his daughter so he took zigzag routes flying across Europe to get home. He took her for the first time to a restaurant, and they sat together celebrating. It was 1939.

"As we sat at the restaurant, he said to me, 'Now my daughter, I am very proud that you have finished school and finished with such high honors—what do you want to become?' I said I wanted to work in intelligence and he answered, 'What the hell! Don't you think three in the family are enough? Do anything but that—what else do you want to do?' He suggested going into sports since I was so good in the field. I was champion in Moscow and of the Soviet Union in track and field. He was so insistent that I forgot about going into intelligence. I entered one of the prestigious institutes called the Institute of History, Literature, and Philosophy. It was called MIFLI, and I was quite happy. I didn't have to take entrance exams because I had graduated from high school with honors.

"I planned to graduate from the history department and probably become a journalist. I was active in the Komsomol, the Young Communist League, and was an organizer. After I was in the Institute for two years the war started, and everything turned around when I volunteered. I had no idea where my assignment might take me."

CHAPTER 4

Family

"MY FAMILY WAS AN interesting mixture. My mother came from a family which was not wealthy, but was not poor. They were not from the peasant class. Her father was a tradesman, and he traveled in the country. With his work, he could afford to rent the log cabin in the country for summer vacations. When World War I started, the family lived at the cottage year round. This was the cottage where I was born, and the area is now within the city of Moscow. My grandfather died shortly after I was born, and my grandmother became the strength of the family though she was illiterate. Mother had a brother and two sisters.

"The family was greatly affected when my father (Zarubin) was assigned to Harbin in China. He and my mother worked for the repatriation of the Russians who had fled the country. Russian family members help each other, and Mother asked her sister, Valentina, and her older brother to come to Harbin to work. My Uncle Fedor was a handsome jocular sort, and I loved him very much. He liked children and would play games with me. My aunt Valentina was an excellent typist, so there was much work for her to do.

"My uncle fell in love with a Russian immigrant in Harbin. They were married and had four children, but when he returned to Moscow he was arrested and put into prison, and we never heard anything about him or his family again. Mother tried to find some record of the family. She knew it was against the law for her brother to marry a Russian immigrant, and she was told that no records were available. It was traumatic, but that was the procedure in those early years of the Soviet Union.

"My Aunt Valentina returned to Moscow and worked in the Ministry of Transport. When she became older she loved to tell fortunes, and that is probably where I got the gift of fortune telling. Later she married a man who became a professor of Chinese language and literature. During his student days he had no place to live, and he would come out and join us for meals at our home. Mother and step-father liked him and helped all they could. This was how he met my aunt and later married her.

"I am not sure what the charges were, but Aunt Valentina's husband was also put into prison. She never did receive notification of acquittal, but she finally received a paper saying that he had died of a heart attack.

"When we returned from Turkey we helped the family in every way we could. There are family traditions in Russia which are binding. Because of Leonid's position we had better rations than others, and we were able to dress better, so Mother was always sharing with her family members. The tradition of family sharing is still very strong in Russia.

"My father, Vasily Zarubin, came from a family of railroad workers. My paternal grandparents had twelve children. My grandmother, Praskovia, died when she was ninety-four. My grandfather was working on the railroad line when it was very cold, and the next day they found him dead—frozen to death at his post. Father was almost fourteen, the oldest at the time, and very eager for education, but he had to assume responsibility for the family. By this time only six of the children were living. My father became a part of the Bolshevik Revolution. He only had a primary education, but he had a beautiful voice. When people would ask him how he learned to sing so well, he would say, 'I don't tell anybody and I don't put it in my personal file, but I learned to sing in the church choir!' His education was also extended in the church.

"In 1920 after my father was in KGB Intelligence, he was also providing for his family. His sister Anna was in KGB, his sister Alexandria was working at the Bureau of Food, and his brother, Sergei, worked for the Moscow District Counterintelligence. He was with the guerrilla detachment around Moscow and was killed by the Germans early in World War II. Another sister, Varvara, was an invalid by this time, and the youngest sister Olympiada married a dental specialist.

"As I was growing up it was a large mixed family. My mother was with Leonid Eitingon, a Jew, and my father married Elizabeth Rosenzweig who came from the southern part of Moldavia, and she was a Jew. She spoke beautiful Romanian, knew English, French, and German and was a key to Zarubin's success in getting strategic information during the war in the United States. We called her Liza and she had five brothers and sisters. It was our tradition for both families to get together often. Russians and Jews, we were indeed a mixed lot. At that time we didn't invite outsiders when we got together because those were dangerous and troubled times.

"Grandmother would sit as the matron and head of the clan enjoying her mixed family. Father, being a man full of good humor, would end the parties by playing the balalaika or the guitar, and we all sang Russian songs. Now none of the Zarubins remain except my half-brother and myself as the senior survivors of the family. My half-brother was born to Liza somewhere in Europe in 1932. He stayed in Switzerland in boarding school while the Zarubins were on assignments for Intelligence.

"My step-father, Leonid, had two sisters and one brother. The family came from Mogilev. His father apparently was an educated man, but he died of an ulcer when he was very young. Leonid was recruited by KGB Intelligence and asked to come to Moscow. He brought his mother, sisters, and brother with him, and they lived in a communal apartment sharing kitchen and bathroom with other tenants on the floor.

"The spirit of family cooperation and sharing got them through rough times. All his sisters and his brother received higher education, and Isaak became a specialist in chemistry. He received many awards because he did research in chemical use on submarines and ships. One sister became a medical doctor, and we always enjoyed having her come for a visit. She talked a lot and told us stories about her work. Leonid was always quiet so Sonya was great fun when she was in our home. She was later put into prison by Stalin during the Doctor's Plot. She was working as the head doctor of the polyclinic of one of the largest plants in Moscow. The other sister, Serafima, became a metallurgical engineer. They were very devoted to their mother. It was a devoted Jewish family.

"I was a teenager at the time, and when the families would get together they would tell me to go take care of the younger children so the grownups could have fun together. We loved those get-togethers, and we were very happy together. There was no difference between Jews and Russians until after World War II when the anti-Cosmopolitan campaign caused strong feelings of anti-Semitism. In 1947 World War II soldiers returning from Berlin wanted changes in Soviet society. When they spoke out about wanting to change and make life better, the Party leadership labeled it Cosmopolitanism.

"Leonid's mother was Evdokia and the family lived close to Red Square. I didn't know about Jewish tradition or about other traditions, but I knew there were special holidays like Hanukkah when special foods were prepared like gefilte fish. Evdokia would cook the special foods with everyone helping to get the hard-to-obtain ingredients. She still lived in a communal apartment with her daughter, Sonya, and Sonya's two children, and when she cooked the holiday foods in the communal kitchen, all the neighbors were interested in the way she was preparing the food. Then we would all get together and enjoy the feast.

"My father's family and my step-father's family were very close, and the relationship continued for many years. I know that my father loved my mother all of his life, and sometimes I could feel undercurrents, but Liza was a very clever woman, and my mother loved Leonid, and he was fond of me and very proud of all that I accomplished.

"There was a long period when I would only see my father as he came from assignments abroad, but he kept in close touch with me. I was fortunate to have two families. One time when Father came back from Europe he brought me a foreign made bicycle. He would always go to grandmother's house in the country and have long walks in the woods to relax.

"Before Leonid and my mother got together he had a son, Vladimir. He always called himself my brother, and we were very congenial.

"Once when I was very young, staying with my grandmother, Evdokia, my father came home from work one day, and I ran to him to tell him about a theater where there were lots of lights and singing. I told him how much I enjoyed it and that they gave me something to eat and drink. My father looked sternly at grandmother and said, 'Now look here, you don't mean to tell me that you took her to church and had her baptized?' Grandmother answered, 'I sure did!' He couldn't scold her in front of me, but he wasn't at all happy. Religion was not accepted by the Party, but Grandmother never accepted the Party. She would take me to services now and then and would talk to me about it without using the word God very much. But she would say, 'I am a believer because we have been believers in my family for a very long time.'

"Somewhere I read recently that before the Revolution, Russians all trusted in God and thought that paradise would come in 2,000 years. But later on their religion became Communism—having equality, sharing everything, living a wonderful and happy life. I had taken it all in along with my school and the activities I was involved in and all of the wonderful, positive people who were our leaders. I was impressed with the loyalty, patriotism, and desire to do good things. But along with all of this, we had fear. I would talk to my grandmother, and she gave me that feeling of belief. My stepfather and mother were always at work so we learned much of our attitude toward people and life from my grandmother. She lived with us until she died in 1936 when I was sixteen. She died of heart failure at the age of 56, but she looked very old to me.

"It was the first time I had to deal with death in my own family. My mother was a very emotional person like my sister and later my daughter. Grandmother died in the hospital and when we found out, Mother told me to go to the morgue and look for her. Mother wouldn't dream of going to the morgue so I went and found her among the corpses. I was really upset because Leonid and my mother had separated, and I had to take care of the arrangements. It wasn't easy for a girl of sixteen.

"My mother had given birth to another little girl, Inna, just three years before, and the baby died when she was only three months old. As a result, my mother was emotionally disturbed and went into a deep depression and didn't talk for six months. Then she wanted to join Leonid on his assignment, but he did not want her to come, and this was a tragic rejection for her. That was when she lost the ability to speak. At that time I was only thirteen, but I really grew up in a hurry because there was no man in the family. My grandmother was living then, but she could not help with problems. She was still trying to do things, but unable to complete them.

"We finally had to get a psychiatrist in, an old gentleman, to work with Mother. He fell in love with her and worked very hard to bring her out of depression and was successful. When Leonid returned in 1934 he asked her to forgive him, but she would not forgive him and told him to leave the home. They had never been officially married. Later, during the war, Leonid was sent to Turkey on assignment to assassinate the German Ambassador von Papen, he met and lived with Musa, a parachutist, and had two children with her. After the war, von Papen was judged as a criminal at the Nuremberg trials.

"In those days as a rule, the majority of couples were never officially registered. They decided to have a common household, and that was enough to be called civil marriage, and you didn't have to register—nobody cared.

"As a matter of fact my mother's birth name was Olga Vasilyeva, and she did not change it until we were in Peking with Leonid. Then she became Naumova because Naumov was one of the names Leonid used in undercover work. His birth name was Eitingon. As an intelligence officer he was given names to be used in special assignments. Mother's passport read Naumova, and though she was never legally registered under that name, she was eventually buried under that name. She and Leonid were separated from 1934 to 1947.

"When we returned from China, my sister got a false birth certificate saying she was born in Perovo (my birth place). In 1927 it would have been unheard of for a Soviet child to have a Chinese birth certificate. In those days you didn't have to have a stamp on your passport. Everything was taken for granted.

"Men and women were more relaxed about relationships. Even though Leonid and my mother were not registered, after they were separated, he always helped the family financially. But by then he had those two children by another woman. I was young, but I felt the responsibility for the whole family. And when she was lying in bed as an invalid in later years, Mother would say to my sister and me, 'My dear girls, I hope you never love a person the way I love Leonid. It is torture!'

"Women could not always control their life situations. The Soviets said women were equal but the reality was that they were anything but equal and had to take things in stride. It is still difficult for me when I think of it because I had no right to judge Leonid. Those two children grew up to be very nice people, but I could never understand how a person as nice as Leonid could get into so many entanglements. He was a good step-father to me.

"During this period Leonid was commissioned to go to Spain for the Civil War. He would send parcels containing mostly clothes and fabrics to make clothes, but Mother would take it to the commissioner's shop and sell it, and then invite her friends to a party. She didn't want his gifts, but she had to take the support money which he always sent by his junior colleagues. He sent letters with the money and said very kind things to each of us. While grandmother was still with us she could help us manage with food. She had relatives in the country who had gardens and grew their own food. It was the time when rationing was very severe. She would go to the country and trade clothes for sacks of potatoes. When she had several sacks of potatoes, she would let us know by telegram that she was coming back on the train, and Leonid would meet her with a car. We would have roasted potatoes and sometimes potatoes in jackets, and we feasted for a while. There was very little meat or chicken, but we had a variety of cereals which grandmother would prepare in different ways by adding some pasta, or plums, or eggs to make it different.

"I was ashamed to go with Grandmother to the market. She would bargain and push and haggle over a few rubles or kopecks. I was embarrassed, but we would put everything together and be able to buy tissue, sugar, and things that were very limited in rationed goods.

"In the early thirties we started having what they called Torgsin shops. It meant trading with foreigners using foreign currency. You had to have gold to trade for the special coupons, but you could get unusual foods that were not on the rationing list. My grandmother sold the few little gold things that she had and got bonds for them. She wore a gold chain and cross which she never sold, but she gave up her wedding ring and other gold jewelry. Once in a while she would give the bonds to my mother and tell her to go buy whatever she wanted. We were very fortunate that we lived through it all because the times were very difficult.

"Once she wanted me to go do the shopping. It was very cold and my shoes were being mended and re-soled. Grandmother let me wear her boots, but they were white so she gave me galoshes to wear over them. It was so crowded in the tram, and I lost one of the galoshes. She really scolded me, and I was hurt. Later I realized that this was the one and only pair of galoshes she had possessed throughout her lifetime so we managed to get another pair of galoshes for her.

"Later in 1944 when my daughter Tanya was very small, she was learning to talk, but she took everything in that was happening around her. She was aware that we could only buy with rationing coupons, and she observed the bargaining. At the time I was going to the KGB specialized school of languages and got special worker's rations because I was an officer. I would collect loaves of bread for two weeks and take them to the market and exchange them for cream cheese, butter, soap, and vegetable oil. Tanya would go with my mother to shop, and one day she said, 'I know you bought me at the market! But what did you sell to get me?' Then she said, 'You are all impostors. I was not bought at the market—I was born but I still don't know how that happened!' No more single words and phrases for her. From then on she talked about everything."

CHAPTER 5

Marriage, Motherhood, and War

ZOYA MARRIED IN 1940 after a very short courtship. She was in her second year at the University. Vasily Minayev had been one of her numerous boyfriends when they were in school No. 50, but he had been away serving in the army. He came home on leave, and she met him quite by chance on the street in July.

She and Vasily had been together in the Youth Sports Club. He was a good athlete—a short distance runner in track and field. Their meeting was a renewal of their friendship. Soon the subject of marriage came up.

His father had been in the Navy before the revolution, but now he was working for the KGB technical service. He was a very nice man and a loving parent to his two sons. Anastasia, the mother, was a homemaker. Zoya had known the father and admired him, but recognized that the mother was always at the beck and call of her husband and sons. The parents were from a very simple, hard working family.

"After Vasily proposed to me, he took me to a party. All the people there knew him, but I didn't know any of them. When he said, 'Meet my wife,' I was surprised, but being a good mixer in a social gathering, I relaxed and danced with several of the men. The hostess came to me and asked, 'What made you marry this person?' Then I told her that we were not married yet. Her response was, 'He is a very good lover, but he will never be a good husband.' It became imprinted in my memory. Vasily watched me dancing with other men, and he didn't like it so we left rather abruptly.

"When my mother and sister were in the country house my family had rented for the summer, Vasily came to the apartment and said that if I didn't marry him, he was going to kill himself. He showed me a revolver.

"I was not in a hurry to marry, but he took me by storm. He was different from the rest—very handsome and dressed in western clothes. He could get them in Western Ukraine on the border where he was stationed. They were something unusual for us to see at the time. When I was out with him, everybody noticed us, and he had a way of paying special attention to me that was disarming. It was wonderful, and I was young and vulnerable.

"My father had just gotten an apartment in Moscow, and when we married on September 6, 1940, he gave the wedding party for the family. There were forty guests, and my father had to take the doors off the hinges to make tables. He bought lots of sausage, potatoes, salad, and drinks. We missed my step-father Leonid who at the time was in Mexico having completed the assignment of eliminating Trotsky. It was accomplished through one of his agents, Ramon Mercader, whom he had recruited in Spain.

"During the party Vasily drank and became very jealous when I danced with other men. When Sudaplatov sat beside me and talked about remembering me from the time I was a small child, my husband became very jealous and angry. His behavior was rough and unacceptable. My step-mother, Liza, noticed his arrogant behavior and ordered a car saying she thought we needed to be together.

"He was very rough with me in the car and threw the Parker pen and pencil set my father had given him at me, saying that I was no good and didn't know how to behave as a wife, then added that he didn't want anything to do with me. It was the middle of the night, and he got out of the car and left. It was my father's car, and I didn't want the driver to be involved, so I got out and walked, too.

A nice gentleman offered me a ride and took me home. An elderly relative who was living with us opened the door and started crying when she saw me alone.

"When I got home, the 100 roses he had given me in the morning for the wedding were there, but he was not. The next morning his father called and brought him back to the apartment. I cried and he cried, and we decided to try and make it work, but his jealousy turned my life into a nightmare.

"We had some time together before he had to return to his post. Due in part to his behavior at the wedding, I realized he was a heavy drinker, and very jealous, and I began to think I had made a mistake. When we would go out, the ladies were all over him, and he paid no attention to me, but got very angry if other men paid attention to me. He was a spirited man because he was so good looking, and everyone catered to him.

"After we married we lived in the apartment with my mother and sister. Some of the gentlemen who came to visit with us had known me since I was a little girl, and they treated me with affection just as they had always done: they would put their arm around my shoulders and kiss me on the cheek. One day after one of these visits, my husband had a jealous fit and called me all of the nasty names he could think of and then said I was a whore. I told him I would never be able to forgive him.

"We had just discovered that I was pregnant, and because our future together looked very grim, I decided to have an abortion. In those days legal abortions were not permitted, but I was determined, and made arrangements for the doctor to come to the apartment. My mother was bitterly opposed to abortion, and she literally got down on her knees and pled, 'Whether you want to live with Vasily or not, please keep this baby. Whatever you do is your business, but give the child to me.' My husband was also crying and pleading with me, and I couldn't look at him because I knew if he smiled, I would forgive everything. He was very persuasive and, in his own limited way, he loved me, though I had no idea what he was doing when he was not at home.

"I continued to study at the University even though it was a very difficult pregnancy. Tanya was born June 2, 1941, three weeks before the War started. I volunteered for the Nurses Corps. My first assignment was to write letters for those who were wounded, and I would often shed tears with them.

"One day as I was going through the lobby, I saw a group of people. They were refugees. There was a very tall Jewish woman holding a baby. She was barefoot, and everyone was gathering around her. I talked to her, and she told me she was running away from the bombing, and while she ran one of the German pilots spotted them, flew low and shot her daughter who was by her side. She got on a freight car and came to Ufa. She said the baby was about three-and-a-half months old, and was starving. I was breast feeding Tanya and had an excess of milk, so I took the baby and fed him with all the people watching. The mother threw herself down and started kissing my feet. I will never forget the experience. I corresponded with the woman for years later. She went back to Minsk in Belorussia. The boy's name was Boris and he became a violinist. She sent a picture of him when he was sixteen. Belorussia is on the western edge of Russia and all of those hundreds of years, when the invaders came, they would come through Belorussia. The people suffered over and over again. They were involved with every invasion except when the Tartars came from the east.

"I continued in the Nurses Corps until my husband was reassigned. Sudaplatov made him his aide-de-camp and sent him to Vladivostok on the East Coast. I decided to try to make the marriage work just one more time so I accepted an assignment from the KGB to go with him as a translator, and as soon as I arrived, I began to translate the documents in the German Consulate. I did not stay very long because the marriage was not working, and it became obvious that it was not going to work out happily. Tanya and I returned to Moscow.

"When I got to Moscow the straps were cut from my bag, and my ID and other items were stolen. That meant that I had to wait another year of probation before I could become a full member of the Communist Party. In 1939 just before I graduated from high school, I had thought I should apply for full membership because I was very active in the Young Communist League. I was recommended by the District Committee of the Komsomol. A number of Leonid's friends gave me recommendations. To become a member it is necessary to have three personal recommendations, and Leonid's friends were important people in foreign intelligence, but

Zoya Zarubina before leaving for Tehran

Zoya Zarubina as guide at Tehran

Meeting hall at Yalta Conference

Churchill, Roosevelt, and Stalin at the Yalta Conference

Zoya Zarubina at Potsdam

Zoya Zarubina at the Crimean Palace Plaque for the Yalta Conference.

Zoya and her Mother, Olga Vasilyeva (1924)

Left: Zoya at age four
Right: Zoya Zarubina as a Pioneer

Zoya Zarubina and Father Vasily in Harbin, China

Zoya swinging at the settlement in China— later occupied by the Chinese army.

Zoya riding her bicycle along the Soviet-American wall

Zoya, Mother Olga, and Svetlana

*Pioneer Club Group, Zoya (second from left) Pioneer Leader Degtyarev
(leading designer of War Planes later).*

Zoya as cross country champion for Dynamo Sports 1938.

Zoya with father Vasily Zarubin.

Zoya's mother, Olga Naumova, 1951

Vasily Zarubin 1937–38.
Photo to be used on
Commemorative Postage Stamp.

Leonid Naumov Eitingon, step-father

Liza Zarubina, step-mother

Zoya and daughter, Tatiana (age 2½)

Tatiana as an adolescent

Peter Zarubin, Zoya's half-brother

Svetlana and Zoya

Zoya and her grandson, Alexei

Leonid Eitingon, step-father,
during World War II.

Eitingon before Stalin
sent him to prison.

Olga, Vladimir Eitingon (son), Zoya, and Eitingon at the Hunting Lodge

Tatiana, Eitingon, Zoya, Olga, and Svetlana

Zoya, Eitingon, and Svetlana

Left: *Zoya when Eitingon was in prison, 1951.*
Right: *Vasily Zarubin (far right) during the Civil War, 1920.*

*Vasily Zarubin (center) and his colleagues in Vladivostok celebrating
his birthday, February 24, 1924. Translation on the side
"To be a superior and a friend is a rare quality."*

Left: *Vasily Zarubin, Civil War, 1922*
Right: *Vasily Zarubin and Liza Zarubina*

Zoya Zarubina and Inez Jeffery
Channel 17 RSVP Program, Austin, Texas, November 4, 1993.

Left: *Vasily Zarubin with daughter Zoya, and granddaughter Tatyana*
Right: *Zoya with daughter Tatiana on Zoya's 75th birthday, April 5, 1995*

Last picture of Vasily Zarubin (center) 1969; (left to right) Anna Zarubina (sister), Liza (wife), General Kondrashov, Zarubin, Colonel Gromuchkin, Zoya and Bernie; (back row standing) Colonel Korznikov, Jenia Zarubina (sister-in-law) and Colonel Ilyin.

Zoya with her father's portrait, April 5, 1995

1961 Woman's Peace Walk with Bobby Fischer's mother delivering a message to Mrs. Khrushchev in Moscow and Zoya interpreting.

before the year of probation was up, I was away on a sports event, and there was no such thing as changing dates or rules. The second time I applied I became pregnant, and now the third time I was to apply my ID and documents were stolen. No ID or documents are replaced without a lengthy process. As a result, I was one of the few candidates who spent six years on probation before I became a full member of the Communist Party. It was like always being in the wrong place at the wrong time."

When Zoya ended her marriage and returned to Moscow and started working as a translator for the KGB, she was translating confidential documents from Germany.

Right from the beginning of the war the people lived from one news broadcast to another. There were loud speakers on poles on top of the building, but at home they were smaller and were made of black paper. Very few people were privileged to have radios.

"We were all glued to those black paper loud speakers which were on a wall or on a table. The news came every hour on the hour, and we all gathered around. Things really got bad when the Germans were approaching Moscow in the middle of October 1941. At that time my step-father, Leonid, and Sudaplatov, head of the Guerrilla Department of the KGB, were very busy preparing guerrilla groups to stay in Moscow in case it should be occupied. This was the time when I had three passports because I was assigned by the military as a patriot, and they would give me one to move from one place to another depending on the action. They registered me as a woman with a child just in case they wanted a conspiratorial apartment. That way there would be an apartment which would be a meeting place for the guerrillas.

"Recently [1993] one of my godchildren told me with great excitement that he had moved into a new apartment, and he was very proud. 'You can't imagine what it is like.' I went for a visit and realized it was the conspiratorial apartment where I had worked with the guerrillas. I remembered the courtyard very well.

"Our leaders planned to blow up many enterprises inside the city because they did not want to leave anything for the enemy. Hitler knew that we celebrated the October Revolution on November 7. The Germans were on the outskirts of Moscow and could see the city through field glasses. No one was sure what was going to happen, but people were mobilized during the night at Mayakovsky

Square. It is on Gorky Street, and there were a number of theaters so there were many chairs available. At night volunteers were asked to bring all of the chairs from the theaters to the Mayakovsky Square underground station—the deepest in Moscow in those days. During the night the chairs were brought down to what had been a raid shelter, and it was turned into a hall where the deputies came and celebrated the 7th of November. It worked very well because Stalin could get there by the underground from his headquarters.

"I was not there, but I helped carry those chairs, and later Leonid told me what it was all about. They brought in a whole train to this station and turned some of the cars into buffets. Stalin gave his speech which was important in those days. It was broadcast across the country.

"The next day people were wondering whether or not there would be a parade as was the tradition on November 7. It was very cold, and sure enough the soldiers came out in the parade. They literally went from Red Square via Gorky Street to the battle front. They crossed Red Square and made a 'U-turn' at St. Basil's Cathedral and continued on Gorky Street to do battle with the Germans.

"It was a scary time because there were days right up to November when up to 10,000 people died each day on the front. Then the Siberian Division came in by train. They were well equipped for the winter, and all of them were trained soldiers. The soldiers we had in Moscow were just young lads—volunteers who didn't know how to shoot well, nor did they have enough rifles or ammunition.

"The commanders were pushing the young soldiers like human fodder. They shouted, 'Hold on! For at least an hour, for at least 30 minutes, but don't retreat!' December 6 became the wonderful day. The trained Siberian soldiers moved in [for] the counteroffensive against Hitler. For the first time since 1939, he faced defeat. It was important for all of the Allies to see that he was not invincible.

"December 5th and 6th were called Moscow Defense Days. Very late on the night of the 5th, they started the counteroffensive and pushed the Germans back some twenty-five kilometers. There was extensive destruction during the occupation. Zoya Kosmodem-yanskaya became the first woman hero of the Soviet Union. She was a guerrilla in warfare. A statue was erected to her.

"She was in one of the villages and was sent to set the barns on fire, but something went wrong in the assignment, and the enemy caught her. It was winter, and they made her walk throughout the night in her underwear. She was just eighteen, but she walked very proudly. They assembled the villagers to see her hanged. She said to them, 'Don't cry—don't be sorry for me because I give my life to my country, and I know we will be victorious. We will defeat them!'

"There is nothing like fighting on the battlefront, but it was in the rear where women did the most to liberate and bring the country to victory. In the rear we had mostly women, and they did all the jobs. Moscow was free but there was still a long way to go. Women worked in every capacity, and we got a lot of lip service from Stalin and other leaders of the country on International Women's Day on March 8th each year. They talked about how wonderfully all women are doing, and that they are our great pride, but it all implied, 'Be patient and we will change things and turn them around so life will be better for you!' We are still waiting, but we have to give our country credit that there are so many good things happening."

There was much idealism in the Soviet Union on the part of all the people and some of the leaders. The Party held a tight rein at all times and successfully disciplined the people according to the Communist's standards and wishes. The people remained loyal to their country, doing what they thought was best for the most people. Many of the people were never aware of all the atrocities being carried on by the leaders in the Party. Families who were touched by the action often disappeared as a unit.

CHAPTER 6

The Years of Tragedy (Eitingon)

In 1951 EITINGON WAS arrested, and Zoya was immediately demobilized and dismissed from the KGB as an intelligence officer. She witnessed the arrest because she had ordered a car and was at the airport to meet him as he returned from his assignment. This time he was flying in from Tallin in Baltic Estonia. When Zoya got to the airport, she was told that the plane had already landed. Because she had her ID and permission she went toward the area. However, the plane taxied to a dark corner of the airfield. She kept walking toward it and when it stopped, she saw Leonid getting off surrounded by men in uniform. She ran toward him, but he was taken in the opposite direction.

She shouted his name and he responded, "Dear Zoya what are you doing here and where is your mother?" She told him that Mother was waiting for him. He shouted back, "Go home!" She took the car and went home knowing something was wrong. There were too many officials involved in getting him off the plane. When she got home she realized that Leonid had been taken into custody.

She did not know how to tell her mother why he was not with her but felt that she must somehow prepare the family for the worst. Her sister was a young student and her own daughter, Tanya, was ten years old. Mother was concerned and Zoya said to her, "He was summoned to the office on urgent business. We'll wait for him and he will be here."

In the middle of the night, the officers came with a warrant to search the apartment. They were abrupt and intent on doing a good job. Zoya relates, "We had a lot of books, and they continued the search for about eleven hours—all through the night and into the next day. They took many papers and all of my pictures from the Tehran Conference. They were surprised that we didn't have a private car and did not have our own *dacha*.

"Mother was in hysterics, very frightened, and didn't seem to understand the situation. As soon as they left, I went straight to the KGB Office and reported what had happened. I had no idea what to do. My boss, Sudoplatov, gave an immediate response, 'Write a report that you want to be demobilized.' I was told by the personnel department that I should wait for the call which would come after they found a civilian job for me. In *Special Tasks*, Sudoplatov stated that I had called him during the evening of the search which would have been impossible. We were not permitted to use the telephone.

"The most difficult period came after I was demobilized and had no income with a family to support. I knew I couldn't wait long because Mother was in a bad state emotionally. I had started my professional life in KGB Intelligence during the war. We lived in a world of our own, in a very large apartment, which was a privilege because Eitingon was considered a hero for his service with the top brass during the war.

"I was a disciplined party member. I knew that being a member of the family of a political prisoner who was accused of treason would change my life and the position of the family. We would be lucky to remain in Moscow. What should I do? What could I do for the rest of the family?

"The second day after the arrest, the door bell rang. When I opened the door a young lady was standing there smiling. She said, 'My name is Muza and I want to talk to you.' She came in and showed me photographs of two children. She was the mother of

Leonid's youngest children. Thank God my mother was not at home. Muza told me that she had an apartment in her own name and that Leonid came to see her and the children now and then, but she hadn't heard from him since he went to Tallin and was concerned.

"I told her about his arrest and asked her not to come to the apartment again. I agreed to come to her and give her any news I received. This was how we met, and I kept in contact with her all during the years he was in prison. Periodically, I took money to her for the children. Leonid was with Muza when he was on assignment in Turkey. She was the champion parachutist.

"One time I asked a colleague who was Dean of the Translation Department at the Institute of Foreign Languages to take me in his car to deliver the money to Muza. I discovered later that he reported me to the KGB implying that I was financially supporting a political prisoner's other family. I was summoned to come to the KGB Office and a colonel who knew me said, 'You need to distinguish your friends from your enemies.' Then he told me that the dean had informed the KGB that I had contacts with the family of a traitor. I had to associate with him at the Institute so I did not say anything, but many years later at a party where we were both guests, I let it be known that I knew people who had betrayed me, and he was very uncomfortable."

The period of waiting for the personnel department of the KGB to find a job for Zoya was devastating. Zoya found herself for the second time in a position to start life anew. The first time was when the war broke out, but now with a family member condemned as a traitor, she had to preserve and protect her extended family. But starting again after Leonid Eitingon's arrest seemed impossible.

In 1951 Stalin sent Eitingon to prison accusing him of participating in a conspiracy to overthrow the Soviet Government and establish a Jewish State. After Stalin's death in 1953, Eitingon was released.

On the fourth day after Eitingon's arrest, family members started visiting prisons trying to find him so they could send parcels. All the families in the same situation went through this painful, humiliating procedure so the lines were long. One waited patiently and then would tell one of the window clerks what day he was arrested and ask if he were there. If the answer was "yes," then the clerk would tell the family that they could bring a parcel and some money once a month. All the families who shared this tragedy were suddenly suspect and were treated as such while they stood in the long lines to get information.

"We knew that Leonid had ulcers of the stomach, and we were worried about him because he was a very sick man. We found him in the Central Lubyanka prison inside the KGB building, but for months and months we knew nothing about him. Waiting for information was agony. Periodically, we went to inquire and were met by information clerks who peered at us from little windows in the wall. We met a drastically different category of people—all women.

"This experience changed my life. I had not realized how privileged my family was. I had the impression that everyone lived the way we did, but now I realized how people could be put down and humiliated every day of their lives. When I stood waiting in those long lines to inquire at the windows, I met people who didn't know who Leonid was and didn't care, but the fact that we had relatives in prison made us friends. We wanted to cling together because we felt that we were the lepers of society. We were the ones who could contaminate the rest.

"The need for a job was uppermost in my mind. My responsibilities had increased, and at the lowest ebb I got a call from the KGB Military Translation School to teach English. This was the school where I had studied during the war, and it was near the KGB building. I went to the school and was there almost a whole day. They showed me the teaching materials and listed my responsibilities. The lady who was chair of the department said that I had been cleared, but at the end of the day I was summoned by a KGB personnel officer only to be told that I was a security risk and could not work in the school. My first thought was that I had been trusted with the most secret assignment in the history of the Soviet Union, and now I was labeled a security risk! They promised to find me another job but I was despondent.

"The next day I went to the Institute of Foreign Languages, where I had worked on a per hour basis, to see Dean Victor Schmidt. I told him I needed a job and asked if they would let me teach. He said, 'You can start now!' But I told him he would have to listen to my story first, and I told him about Leonid's imprisonment. His response was, 'Is that all that worries you? Many of us are in the same position. Forget that you have someone in prison and come to work—we need you now.'

"The next day I went to the KGB intelligence personnel to ask if they had found a position for me. I knew I had to follow procedure because I had not been officially dismissed. I was told that they had found a job, and I was to be head of the Chancellery of the Dynamo Sports Stadium because I was an athlete and knew languages, and they were anxious to start corresponding with foreign sports organizations. I would be ideal for the translations. They told me that in this post I would deal with the correspondence.

"I thanked them but told them that I already had a job. When they asked what it was I declined to answer, but was happy as I walked out of the office because I knew that a new stage of my life as a civilian had begun. I became an English language teacher in the evening school on December 5, 1951. I felt good because I had taught there two years while I was in intelligence and had the cum laude diploma so I could feel at home in the civilian teaching field. I planned to look for students who wanted private lessons and knew that I could make it.

"One day in early March of 1953, I felt an urgent need to get home. I called but the line was busy so I got organized and left the Institute. When I got home, Leonid was sitting in the dining room with Mother, my sister, and my daughter Tanya. Stalin died the 5th day of March, and Leonid told us that Beria sent his Deputy Minister Bogdan Kabulov to Leonid's cell to bring him to his office so he could tell him that he was free. My first thought was that Beria needed him very much for special covert operations. It took a couple of days to prepare the necessary papers and two officers escorted Leonid home. Mother told me that when he rang the doorbell the officers were standing behind him with all of his decorations and medals.

"When my mother saw him she threw herself on him, and they both fell because he had lost forty-two kilos [ninety-three pounds]. He told us that they had tortured him by not letting him sleep. There were electric lights pulsating twenty-four hours a day. Because of his ulcers, he couldn't eat the prison food so there was little to sustain him. He did not complain. He thanked me and whispered into my ear thanks for helping the other woman and her children. Beria assured him that he and his family would be fully reinstated.

"He told me that he was also assured that his son, Vladimir, who was living in Voronezh, and I could be reinstated. I refused reinstatement because I had been through all of the stages of hell I could take. I knew I was forever finished with KGB intelligence; I told Leonid that I was very comfortable at the Institute and wanted to continue the work I was doing. He called Vladimir, and he accepted reinstatement, but in four months Leonid was put into prison again. When Khrushchev had Beria arrested, tried, and shot, Vladimir was dismissed again. He had enjoyed only four months of dignity. The district party committee found a job for him as foreman in a plant where a team of women were manufacturing the wrappings for rice and sugar."

During his months of reinstatement and privilege, Leonid arranged for a voucher so Zoya, and her friend Valentina, could have a vacation at a good *sanatorium* (vacation housing for workers) on the Black Sea where she could swim to her heart's content. Valentina had been a radio operator during the war, and the women enjoyed dancing, singing, and swimming. It was completely relaxing; a world apart from what they had been experiencing.

On the day they returned to Moscow, all was well. Zoya went to the market and bought a big watermelon. As she came into the house she knew things were not right. She had seen a number of cars in front and as she went toward the elevator, she saw unfamiliar men milling around. When she got into the apartment there were ten men around Leonid. He had been arrested again—this time by Khrushchev, and Eitingon would be in prison for ten more years.

Zoya was grateful that she had not given in to Leonid's pressure to be reinstated into KGB intelligence when he was liberated after the first two years in prison. His son, Vladimir, who did accept reinstatement, would be kicked out again and go through the trauma of no status and perhaps no job.

Zoya says that as Leonid was leaving the apartment with the officers he said to her, "I am so sorry, and I appreciate all that you did for the family. I hope you will keep it up." She understood that he meant the additional members of the family, and she assured him that she would take care of them.

She had some advice for Vladimir this time. She was direct in telling him not to be stupid about waiting for the Party to help him, but go for higher education at the University and prepare for a profession instead of a manual job. He was able to go back to his old job supervising at the paper packaging factory, and he applied to the University Economics Department. He stayed with it until he earned his Ph.D. and became professor and dean of the Economics Department. Now he often travels abroad to participate in international conferences. The Russian government frequently consults with him. He expresses gratitude to Zoya for pushing him toward a profession even though it was difficult to start over.

Leonid returned to prison in July 1953. Once again the family was left wondering why he was arrested. Later they found out that he was accused of being a close associate of Beria and one of his accomplices. He was accused of doing whatever Beria told him to do no matter how cruel or wicked. As head of the KGB, Beria's orders could not be questioned. This time he was arrested with his boss, General Sudoplatov. He had also been Zoya's boss in Intelligence and she helped his son, Anatoli, get into the Institute of Foreign Languages and adjust to life as "the son of a traitor."

Leonid's sentence was for twelve years, and the investigation took more than four years which was a violation of all laws. During that period his family was not allowed to see him, but they could take limited parcels and a little money to the prison for him.

"During our first meeting with him, after four years, we found out that he would be sent to Vladimir, a city north of Moscow, and he was in the same section with Vasily Stalin . . . The prison was known to be one of the most rigid in the Soviet Union. The walls were very thick. The building was built by the Czars for political prisoners. Here the family could visit him once a month, and this was when they took the food parcels. My mother would collect food items for him and do special preparation. She was always worried about his health. I knew that as long as Mother was kept busy thinking about the visit and preparing special food, she would feel better. She had two serious heart attacks, but she was energized by thinking about what to buy and prepare for Leonid from one visit to the next.

"She would often humiliate herself before the women at the little windows who received the parcels. The limit was 10 eggs but Mother would plead, 'Please take 40 eggs, you see he is a sick man, and he needs more eggs!' She would do anything to get the food he needed in to him. We always sent him bandages because he was badly wounded during the Civil War and had a bad leg. Often he was in great pain and needed special bandages. Our family lived from month to month and tried to be as cheerful as possible on the day of the visit. I would hire a car because the prison was far out. It was costly, but it was the only way we could get there. Usually there were five of us in the car—Mother, my sister Svetlana, one of Leonid's sisters, myself, and sometimes Tanya, my daughter."

Leonid also sent a letter to the family each month. They were wonderful letters, but they were letters of a staunch Communist who believed in the system. He tried to cheer them up from his prison cell by saying how wonderful life was and that the country was marching right along. Zoya never asked him if he got any radio news or ever saw a newspaper, but she remembers one letter he sent to her personally. It was on the fortieth anniversary of the October Revolution, and he wrote about how proud he was that his children had lived to celebrate this anniversary. He also told her he was proud that she was a Communist and working for the UN Language School. After he was out of prison, Zoya says that he never spoke with resentment toward either the government or Stalin or Khrushchev. But she knew for sure that he had his own clear cut vision of the progress being made by the Soviet Union and held no resentment.

"After my mother died, and Leonid married a former partner in Intelligence, he saw my grandson, Alexei, for the first time. We were very happy that they could meet, and I introduced Leonid to Alexei as his great-grandfather, the General I have told you about. Above Leonid's bed there was a small framed photograph of Stalin, and as I talked about Alexei wanting to be a general and his interest in the history of the Second World War, Leonid pointed to the picture of Stalin and asked Alexei, 'Who is that?' Alexei said that he didn't know. Leonid responded, 'What kind of a military man are you going to be if you don't know this man? This man is Stalin, a great leader of our country!'

"Leonid had a special feeling for Stalin and how he had made the country strong, but he was an introvert and kept more of his feelings to himself. Many years before, I had ordered a special portrait of Stalin as a gift for his fiftieth birthday in 1950 and had it beautifully framed. When he was arrested the first time the officers were surprised that he had such a nice portrait of Stalin in an expensive frame.

"After Leonid was sent to Vladimir, during the second prison term, he became very ill. His ulcers caused him to feel badly most of the time, but this time it was different. Later we learned that it was a tumor in his colon. Because he was so ill, I began to explore the possibilities of getting a surgeon to operate on him. Through contacts with high ranking generals who took risks to help me, I was able to get an unprecedented permit allowing a leading cancer surgeon to come to the prison and perform surgery. Leonid's sister, Sonya, was a therapist, and she persuaded Professor Mints to do the surgery. Without the generals who were willing to take the chance to get the permit, and Professor Mints' high regard for Sonya, the surgery could not have been performed in the prison hospital, and Leonid would have died."

Family members had to learn to live with the stigma of having a member in prison as a political traitor. Friends no longer dared associate with them. If they saw people they knew walking toward them, they expected them to cross the street or lower their heads as if they didn't recognize their former friends and neighbors. It was a painful experience, but Zoya was inspired by a new circle of friends in her civilian job. Many of them had no inkling of her family tragedy. Those who did accepted her as a professional equal—not as one with a tarnished family.

The family members were daily reminded of their position. Zoya's sister, Svetlana, was in love with a young man who spent a great deal of time in the apartment, but left her as soon as he learned about Leonid's arrest. Now he is a leading poet in Russia and well-known for his popular song lyrics that have become hits.

Because of the isolation, Zoya's mother was most impressed with a gentleman who continued to come to the apartment to see Zoya. Her association with him went back to the Tehran Conference. During that time there were several men in civilian clothes who were actually officers in the KGB, and he was one of them. In Tehran he was supposed to serve as liaison for Zoya helping her to get needed furniture in place and making arrangements for President Roosevelt's apartment. He fell in love with her and became a burden for a number of years. There were times when he literally stalked her.

After Leonid's arrest he continued to come to the apartment and soothe Zoya's mother by talking about the good old times and

having a drink with her. She became very fond of him, and he court-
ed her approval by bringing Georgian fruit and wine that the family couldn't afford. Mother would pressure Zoya and insist that
since he was so much in love with her, she should marry him. Zoya
knew that he was married, but that didn't seem to bother him. The
pressure became so intense, Zoya reasoned, "I don't love anybody.
I am a widow, and if I accept his offer of courtship, I won't have to
run and scratch for every ruble to take care of the family. I am paying a big sum for rent in this big, wonderful apartment which
Leonid received as a World War II hero, but he is no longer receiving benefits, and I am not entitled to benefits because I'm working
in a civilian job."

Zoya reminisced about the period. "I was grateful that we were
living in the 50s because the family could not have remained in the
apartment when times were different. Had it been in the 30s they
would have all been sent to a concentration camp. By working extra
hours at the institute and teaching private lessons, I could pay the
high rent which the government demanded.

"I kept reasoning that for the family's sake I should marry this
man, but I didn't love him, and I finally told him that it was not
possible. He continued to come as if nothing had happened. The
pressure from Mother continued because he kept talking to her
when I could not be at home.

"Much later, when I was dean of the English department at the
Institute, I faced an unprecedented and dangerous situation. A lady
named Elena came to my office one day on business. She said that
she wanted to have a confidential talk with me. She asked me if I
had any enemies, and I responded that I really didn't know because
I hadn't been at the Institute long enough to make enemies. Then I
added that there might be enemies of my father or step-father
because I had not been in a position at KGB to make enemies. I had
served as an interpreter and translator.

"She told me that the Minister had received an anonymous letter about me (which usually meant condemnation without trial). I
immediately thought of the KGB Colonel who had stalked me from
1943 to that moment in 1955 when I rejected him so I told her the
story. I told her that he was very angry when I rejected him but continued to visit with my mother. He demanded that I return his gifts
which amounted to a few trinkets, and I gathered them up and gave
them back to him.

"This coincided with the time when I was renewing my acquaintance with Bernie Cooper, my second husband-to-be, and I am sure the Colonel knew about our association.

"Elena, who was in intelligence, told me some of the content of the anonymous letter which included a warning to beware of that woman; she is the daughter of a political traitor and is corrupting students as the dean of the department by telling them negative things about the Soviet Union. There was much more, but I never saw the letter.

"For several years men who were friendly with me would be approached and warned not to have contact with me again because I was the relative of a traitor and a traitor myself under surveillance, and association with me would affect their careers. They withdrew. Bernie was working with me on sports radio because I was a member of the National Soviet Olympic Committee and was writing a doctoral dissertation on *Language Peculiarities of Sports Terminology*. Because of this association Bernie had been approached with the accusations. When he asked me if I had trouble with anybody, I knew he had been approached. Later I learned the sneaky KGB Colonel had tried to blackmail him and his wife. They were separated, but not divorced, and the wife was told that her husband was keeping company with a dangerous woman.

"In this rare case the Colonel was dismissed from the KGB in disgrace because Elena had followed through and exposed his history and activity. I was sure he would come and take revenge, but he never did."

For years and years acting upon anonymous letters was an everyday procedure in the Soviet Union. Many loyal, good people suffered. Nobody bothered to find out who the "well wishers" were who wrote the letters. Instead they would set up official commissions and (sometimes for months) would search for proof of the alleged facts. If they could confirm twenty percent of the statements they would declare the accusations proved. It was a very painful process for many people.

There were other anonymous letters accusing Zoya of taking bribes as dean at the Institute. Fortunately the officials knew that when they were ordered to follow up on letters they could brush them aside. Many times such letters were based on jealousy or the desire for revenge. The Party Committee would follow through and take these letters seriously even though they were all signed "Well Wisher." This negative practice is disappearing, but still exists. Some Russians who immigrate to the U.S. still resort to such letter writing to the American authorities.

Zoya responded to the Colonel's spying through the years by saying, "It's only when you get older and look back that you realize how terrible some of those things were. At the time we didn't realize because our urge was to survive." She suspected when the Colonel first started visiting her apartment that he was assigned by the KGB to keep a check on the family. That was another reason she did not totally reject his attention earlier. Somehow she felt that this was not the worst choice for supervision.

"One day my secretary came into my office at the Institute to tell me that I had a visitor. She gave me the name of the Colonel. My first thought was that he wanted to get even and might spray some poison on me or do something drastic and harmful. I asked the assistant dean to stay nearby and, just in case anything happened, to be ready to catch him at the door.

"When he came in, I smiled as if nothing had ever happened. I tried to be nonchalant but his first words were, 'I came to apologize for what I've done to you!' Innocently, I said that I didn't know what he had done but he continued, 'I want you to know that your friends were loyal, they did not betray you. They were very good but I was bad to you!' I commended him for coming to apologize, but repeated that I did not know what he had done. I was not about to fall into a trap that would betray those who had come to my rescue. This was the end of that tragic episode, and the KGB attitude toward me changed drastically. Elena has cleared so much for me with the KGB. They even seemed sorry that they had dismissed me because they knew I was doing a good job and was just as much of a patriot as ever. I was loyal to my country and I always will be.

"The KGB reopened the files and cleared me for travel abroad again. In 1952 I had gotten clearance for one trip to the Helsinki Olympics because they needed me to represent the country. I was elected honorary secretary for the Women's Commission of the International Amateur Athletic Federation and worked in that capacity from 1952 until 1968. But it was not until 1955 that the KGB took me off the freeze and trusted me to go out of the country, and that I would not defect. At last I was free once again to come and go, and I started traveling with delegations.

"When everything was going well again, Elena came to see me one day and expressed her pleasure that I had started a new life and was doing so well. Then she told me that she wanted to do something else for me which I deserved. She said that it was a shame that a person of my stature and knowledge of languages was not going abroad to represent the country in a professional way. She was concerned that others were going who had none of the impressive skills. So I knew she was responsible when the KGB lifted the barrier, and I was assigned to go with a delegation to India in 1955 for a lengthy stay—the first time I had been out of the country since Leonid's arrest. By now I was Dean of the English Language Department at the Moscow State Pedagogical Institute of Foreign Languages.

"In spite of all the positive things that were happening, I knew that I had one more very difficult task to perform. Leonid's health was failing in prison, and I knew he couldn't survive much more of the rugged prison life. I wanted to work out a way to get his first time in prison counted so he could get out a year and a half earlier. I decided to take the chance and plead with Colonel General Borisoglebsky, Chairman of the Military Procurator's office, to let his first one and-a-half years in prison under Stalin count so he could be released. I asked for his help because Leonid was a very sick man who had major surgery in the prison hospital and continued to be in the hospital most of the time. He did help me, and Leonid returned home in November of 1964.

"In 1953, Leonid had to be in a rehabilitation hospital for a while, and I visited him regularly. There were other generals there who would tell me how amazed they were that I came often to see Leonid. Then they told me that some of their children had denounced them because they were afraid for their careers. 'You cannot imagine how we felt when we learned about your visits to your step-father, who is also a Jew!' There were a number of high ranking KGB generals, most of them Jews, who had been accused by Stalin as a part of the plot to overturn the government and found a Jewish state.

"I loved Leonid and had great respect for him and what he was doing. He was always thoughtful and good to me as a part of the family. There was no reason why I should not stand by him when he needed me.

"When he came home the situation was very difficult because he had not been acquitted of the charge of political treason. He was told that he could not live in Moscow and would have to report to the police station every week. This humiliating procedure went on for some time. Nobody wanted to look back at the accusation that put him in prison in 1951. Added to that he was mentioned in a closed Central Communist Party letter in 1953 which accused Beria of high treason and named Eitingon as his accomplice. Both Leonid and Sudoplatov were quoted in the letter. In order to reverse the indictment, the endorsement of the Political Bureau was needed. When I appealed for help I was told that only members of the Political Bureau could bring the subject up to reopen the case, and none of them were willing to do it.

"So my step-father had to continue to report to the police station [Militia] weekly. Even though he was not permitted to live at home for a while, we finally did get some of his pension. It was not his major general's pension but that of a soldier—12 rubles and 50 kopecks which was just enough to buy 10 packages of cigarettes. Leonid was a chain smoker. My dilemma was in thinking through the next step that had to be taken. I was the only member of the family who could work on these problems. I suddenly felt the weight of additional responsibility with so many people dependent on me.

"I had to check laws and attempt to bend some of them to survive. Alexander Shelepin was chairman of the KGB, and he was my good friend since our student days before the war. At that time he was secretary of the Komsomol Organization of the Institute, and I was a member of the Committee on Sports, so we had become very good friends. Now so many years later I found a way to contact Shelepin, and he helped me get the papers for a civilian old age pension for Leonid. I had to bribe some functionaries to get all the necessary papers, but I called Shelepin again and asked him how I could put everything together to get a normal pension for Leonid.

"I told him that Leonid was 64 years old, in prison for 12 years, a very sick man, but he has to subsist. I pled that he deserved more than a soldier's pension of 12 rubles. He gave me a clue which I followed. First, we had to find a job for Leonid, and if he stayed at that job for more than a month, he could then apply for a civilian old age pension at his place of employment.

"I had to pay a bribe to get him a position as translator in one of the publishing houses. I knew people who could have done it without a bribe, but everyone was afraid to touch it, especially since Leonid Eitingon had become a notorious name linked with Beria. The contact was a publisher I knew, and I knew his wife collected bone china. I still had a few treasures left so I offered her my bone china, and she gave it a very prominent place in her collection. The publishing house was very happy with Leonid's work and, instead of keeping him a month according to the agreement, he was with them almost two-and-a-half years.

"Leonid became a member of the collective where he worked. He was no longer an ex-convict, but a civilian who was employed and lived at home. His pension increased to 120 rubles plus what he received as a translator, translating from Spanish and French into Russian.

"By this time my mother was a very sick person. She had been in bed for several years after having four heart attacks. As an invalid she was dependent and constantly complaining. It was very painful to see my lovely mother, for whom I had practically given my life, changing so drastically. She just couldn't take the injustices. The younger members of the family coped with the tragedy as best they could. I said very little because I had to cater to each member of the family.

"Mother died in December 1966—a little more than two years after Leonid's return. I had moved from the big apartment, where Leonid was arrested, and Mother became an invalid. We were in smaller quarters, but Mother had asked her sister to come live with us and take care of her while we were still in the large apartment. Aunt Valentina was very good with her, and I'm sure she remembered so long ago when Mother had her come to Harbin, China, to work. My sister Svetlana, her husband, two children, and his sister, who was a student, were with us at the time. It was a crowded home when you counted my daughter, Tanya, and myself. I was also financially responsible for Muza and the two children Leonid fathered with her.

"I didn't give them money monthly because I couldn't afford that, but periodically I gave them money until Leonid was able to do it. I did pass information to them about Leonid before he was released. They couldn't visit him because they were not on the official list as members of the family. Neither my Mother nor my sister knew of my contact with them.

"When Leonid came back, I knew he visited with them, and I was sure that when my mother died he would go back to Muza and the children. He didn't say much, but he was grateful for all that I had done for him."

Eitingon told Zoya that if she were alone, without family, and not married he would stay with her. By this time, however, she had Bernie. Leonid wanted to leave because he had spoiled so much of her life and made things so difficult for her over the years.

To Zoya's surprise, he did not go back to Muza, but renewed a relationship with Yevgenia Puzireva. Zoya says that he was not a man who would go out and get acquainted with someone new, so it was easier to reestablish his relationship with Yevgenia when he met her again at a reunion of veterans from the Spanish Civil War of 1936-1937. She was a veteran of that war too, and he didn't have to explain his situation to her. She invited him into her home for visits.

"He used to tell Mother that he was going for long walks, and I was sure that those were the times he went to see Yevgenia Puzireva and have tea and conversation. After being in prison for twelve years, he needed release from the emotional tension of Mother's illness."

When he decided to leave Zoya's family, he went to Yevgenia. They had much in common after their experience of working together during the Civil War in Spain. He lived with her until his death in 1981.

Yevgenia worked under Leonid's command during the Civil War in Spain. Later she was the only Soviet woman who was decorated with a British military medal for her role in assisting convoys from Britain to the Soviet Union during World War II on the Murmansk run.

Leonid lived with only one thought in mind; how to be rehabilitated which would restore his rank and status. He believed in the Bolshevik Revolution and was a great patriot. It was hard for him to face constant humiliation because of his imprisonment. Zoya placed his application for rehabilitation with high ranking officials while she was head interpreter of the Party Congresses and had easy access to the Presidium. She knew the people who would put his application on top of the stack for Mr. Brezhnev to consider.

The Party Congress met every five years, but the answer always came back that there were no grounds to reopen the case. When he wrote to other organizations, they would answer, "The moment you are reinstated in the Party, that will be a signal for us to reopen the case."

Unfortunately it never happened in his lifetime. Shortly before his death, he became very ill. The authorities placed him in the prestigious Kremlin Hospital near Moscow. There they treated him as an old veteran of the Intelligence service. Even then he was a man of humor and told them not to probe him deeply because he was an old person. His will kept him alive for several years. He was eighty-one when he died in May 1981.

"There was a telephone call from the Central Committee of our Communist Party letting me know what a wonderful person he was and how proud I should be of him. Then they said, 'Do you know how much he did for the country?' I wanted to scream!

"When we went to Leonid's cremation there were about 100 people. Many of his former associates came, but everyone was afraid to speak out. They just stood there looking at me. I knew many of them during the war. Through their looks they acknowledged their sorrow, but they were afraid to open their mouths. Only Colonel Mirkovsky, a hero of World War II, had the courage to speak up at the memorial service. He spoke admirably of Leonid, and then I spoke, but no one else.

"Afterwards, when some people came to Leonid's home to have drinks, many of them then said how much they had loved him and that he had been a wonderful boss. They apologized for not speaking at the memorial service and explained that they were afraid of repercussions. They knew he had not been acquitted.

"Leonid was finally acquitted, thanks to the efforts of his former colleagues and Alexander Yakovlev, the Chairman of the Party Rehabilitation Committee. Yakovlev was one of the assistants to Gorbachov, who was responsible for opening up the secret memoranda of Molotov and Ribbentrop and initiating *Glasnost* and *Perestroika*, which started Soviet openness. Yakovlev also stood for the secession of the Baltic Republics.

"Yakovlev took the time to get our application out of the stack and push it through the Committee. There were thousands and thousands of applications to be considered.

"The acquittal letter was very carelessly written on the letter-head of the prosecutor's office. It stated the dates Leonid was in prison (the dates were wrong), and it showed no grounds for the arrest. No other information was included. There was no apology and no expression of regret.

"The acquittal did not come until April 1992—forty-one long years after his first arrest and twenty-eight years after his final release from prison. Leonid had been dead eleven years before he was cleared of all accusations and rehabilitated."

CHAPTER 7

Vasily Zarubin as Father and Patriot

ZOYA LIVED WITH HER mother and step-father, but had a close and loving relationship with her father. He did not hesitate to advise her. Although he had objected to her getting involved in intelligence work, when she became an interpreter for military intelligence during the war, he supported her in every way. Zoya thought of him as a friend and role model. He taught her to swim and be an athlete. He himself was an accomplished athlete and musician. He would occasionally surprise his family and friends when he would come in his general's uniform and take a chair and stand upside down on it as a greeting.

He played the guitar, balalaika, and piano. After the Russian Civil War he played in many concerts and would accept food for his family as compensation. Zarubin was a lover of nature and would take Zoya for long walks in the woods to pick mushrooms. She missed him when he was away for long periods, but it was always a joyous reunion when he came back to Moscow. She frequently says, "I am proud to be his daughter."

Zarubin fought at the front during World War I from 1914 to 1917, but he was against the war and was sent to a penal squad for his propaganda activities. He was wounded in March 1917 and was given treatment in a hospital in Voronezh. In 1918 he joined the ranks of the Red Army and fought with them on the fronts of the Russian Civil War until 1920. Beginning in 1929 he spent several years undercover in France recruiting supporters for the Soviet Union among the anti-fascist activists. He had an alias and a cover story as a Czech engineer with a forged American citizenship.

During the years that Vasily Zarubin lived under cover in different countries before WW II, he assumed different names with false passports. He was an officer on the KGB staff, and all of the time counted for his retirement.

After the Russian Civil War, he was named chief of the Economic Department for Intelligence and was sent to Vladivostok on the East coast where he led the fight against narcotics and firearms coming in from Europe and China. Later he was transferred to foreign intelligence and sent to Harbin, China, but in 1926 he was recalled to Moscow for another assignment. In the late 1920s he met Liza and married her. She was also an agent with the advantage of being beautiful and clever. They were sent as a team to Denmark where they arrived with Czech passports and succeeded in setting up an illegal residency to be used against Germany. They worked as a husband and wife team for the rest of their lives.

After just two years in Denmark, Zarubin was called for a meeting in Switzerland where he was told he had been appointed to be overseer of illegal intelligence in France. At first he went to the south of France to the small resort town of Antibes to get accommodations. Here he became acquainted with a young French student named Maya. Later on he enlisted Maya and her family, who lived in Paris, to cooperate with the illegal residency and become caretakers of it as a safe house for other intelligence personnel who worked in France.

When the work was well organized in Antibes, Zarubin moved to the Paris suburbs where Liza joined him. They became friends with the owner of the garage where Zarubin kept his car. In a short time Zarubin invested in the garage and became a partner. The garage partner arranged a permanent residence for the Zarubins. Through a Polish agent, whose brother was the owner of an advertising agency in Paris, Zarubin was able to invest in the advertising agency. This created great opportunities for conducting intelligence work and helped him later to establish himself in Germany.

They remained in France until 1933. He headed up the illegal residency which received documented materials about the policy of France toward the Soviet Union. He also secretly obtained important political and economic information from the German Embassy in Paris. When Hitler came into power in Germany, neighboring countries became threatened and feared the possibility of a second World War.

In 1934 Zarubin and Liza were sent to Berlin to head up an illegal residency. He conducted a series of valuable foreign recruitments, successfully supervised the illegal residency, and added great force and energy for the creation of anti-fascist groups. He sent pertinent information to Moscow about Hitler's policy and plans. In 1937 he was awarded the Order of the Red Banner for carrying out the special tasks of his government. This was also the time when Stalin began his great purges.

Shortly after his report Zarubin had an urgent call to return to Moscow. He arrived with his colleagues and recent young recruits. He was immediately summoned by L. Beria, the people's Commissar of Soviet State Security, and accused of being a German spy collaborating with the Gestapo. According to the recollection of eyewitnesses Zarubin answered the "iron commissar" with great dignity and conducted himself as a man certain of his correctness and innocence. Because of his courage and judgment he avoided repression for himself and his family. After all of his years of experience and successful work as an intelligence officer, Beria reduced him to an apprenticeship, then assigned him to teach young recruits.

In spite of Beria's downgrading Zarubin in the spring of 1941, the intelligence center desperately needed his expertise and experience. Thus he got the assignment of going to China to establish contact with a high ranking German advisor to Chiang Kai-shek whom he had recruited when working in Germany. He was able to make contact and learned about the plans Hitler was making for war with the USSR. The advisor was even able to tell him that the plans were to attack in May or June. He immediately sent this information to Stalin who interpreted it as another misinformation ploy. He ignored it as he did similar signals sent by other agents abroad.

He made the arbitrary decision that the war would come much later and would last no more than three months.

In the fall of 1941 Beria summoned Zarubin and took him to Stalin who told him that he would be going to the United States. Zarubin was to make sure that the United States did not sign a treaty leaving out all consideration of the Soviet Union and to probe whatever might be new in the development of armaments. Liza was assigned to go with him. Their work involved a lot of traveling and bringing Soviet cultural programs to the United States. All the while they recruited Americans who were sympathetic to the Soviet Union and the cause of socialism. Liza was an experienced intelligence officer and a very good recruiter. She knew languages and was a good social mixer. Her talents were important to them as a team, and all the information they acquired was sent directly to Moscow and the State Defense Committee.

Many stories have been written about Vasily Zarubin. He was resident Vice Consul and head of Soviet Intelligence at the Soviet Embassy in the United States in the early forties. In rank, he was the most important officer after the Ambassador. Zarubin's position while in the Soviet Embassy was an example of how a diplomatic official can also be an important official of the Soviet Military Intelligence.

Zarubin stayed in the United States until 1944. During his residency he was able to get valuable information which resulted in strengthening the economy and military might of the Soviet Union. He not only directed the residency in the Soviet Embassy, but took an active part in recruitment work. He established a strong network in the United States to gain information on any and all activities that related to the war including the production of the atomic bomb. The information he and Liza obtained from governmental, political, and scientific circles was highly praised in Moscow.

Unexpectedly in 1944 Zarubin was pronounced *persona non grata* by the United States because of an anonymous letter sent to J. Edgar Hoover, FBI director. It accused him and Liza of being Russian agents and also of spying for Japan and Germany. He was expelled from the United States. On returning to Moscow he was "put on hold" for six months and investigated by a special commission. The letter to Hoover was written by Mironov, an aid to Zarubin. He repeated the offense by writing an accusatory letter to

Beria stating that Zarubin was spying for Japan and Liza for Germany. Zarubin was acquitted, and Mironov was placed in a mental institution diagnosed as a schizophrenic. For his achievements Zarubin was promoted to Major General on July 9, 1945. He was named Deputy Chief of Foreign Intelligence and continued in the position until 1948 when he entered the reserve for health reasons. His only benefit for his years of loyalty was that he retained his full pension. Nonetheless he was broken in spirit. This turn of events was especially galling for a man whose work in intelligence was of the highest quality. He was awarded two Orders of Lenin, two Orders of the Red Banner, the Order of the Red Star, and many other honors.

There has been much speculation about his activities in the United States during the period when the Atomic Bomb papers secrets got into Soviet hands. Currently he is being honored in print and film for his outstanding intelligence service over a long period. A number of United States intelligence workers have researched his work while he was in America. Yet with all the power he had while serving as the top intelligence officer in the Soviet Embassy, relatively little has been proven about the work which brought him honors in the Soviet Union.

Zoya disputes the information given in *The FBI-KGB War—A Special Agent's Story* by Robert J. Lamphere and Tom Schachtman. It purportedly tells the story about Zarubin's work in the United States and reports that he died an alcoholic. They refer to him as Zubilin which was an alias and write about his birth name of Zarubin as an alias. He drank very little in his retirement years.

Zarubin's wife, Elizaveta, always known as Liza, was born in 1900 in the Chernovintskaya area of Tzarist Russia, currently independent Moldavia. Her father was the director of forestry on the estate of the landlord, Gayevskiy. The family was quite well-to-do which allowed Liza to complete the Gymnasium (high school) in Chernovitsy. Later she studied with the historical and philological faculties of the Chernovitsy, Paris, and Vienna universities. Besides her native Romanian, she mastered Russian, German, French, and English. She became a member of the Austrian Communist Party in 1923. From 1924 until 1925 she served as translator for the USSR political and trade representatives in Vienna. Her revolutionary experience and knowledge of several European languages, as well as her grasp of the principles of conspiracy, brought her to the attention of foreign intelligence. In 1925 she became an officer of State Security and for three years worked in the Vienna residency. From 1925 to 1928 she recruited several important sources of information into Soviet foreign intelligence work.

For a period of thirteen years she worked with Zarubin in Denmark, Germany, France, and the U.S. She not only assisted him with his work, but also conducted her own intelligence activities. Her work characterized her as a resourceful and energetic intelligence officer who displayed exceptional dedication. In April 1941, by order of the Center, she entered Germany to reestablish contacts with the wife of a prominent Nazi diplomat who had been recruited by Liza in France. Later this source provided important information about Germany during the war. After completing this task for the Center, Liza was instructed to establish contact with a German intelligence agent who was working as a code clerk in the Nazi Ministry of Foreign Affairs. The contact was surprised to see her in Berlin because the war against the USSR was scheduled to start any day. The results of this contact were reported to Moscow.

From 1941 to 1944 Liza worked with her husband on the assignment to the U.S., where she maintained clandestine contact with approximately two dozen agents. They included some of the most valued sources of information who served at the top level of authority. She also recruited new people into the project. From 1944, when she returned to Moscow with Zarubin, until 1946 she worked in the Central Office of Intelligence in Moscow. In September of 1946 she was sent into reserve without a pension at the age of forty-six, obviously because she was Jewish.

In the summer of 1968 Zarubin rented a house far out from Moscow in the deep woods where he enjoyed nature. One day Zoya received a frantic call from Liza telling her that her father had a stroke while walking in the woods to the store. He had lain there unconscious for more than an hour. Zoya immediately called his doctor who insisted that they bring him back to the city as quickly as possible. It was impossible to get an emergency car through because there were no roads adequate enough to guarantee safe passage to the hospital. Zoya arranged for the suburban train to stop long enough for Zarubin to be carried aboard. Her next problem was getting him to the local station from the distant village. She appealed to her students of the United Nations Language Training Center to accompany her to the remote village and carry him on a stretcher for some distance to the train stop. Ten students volunteered and they carried him through the woods and onto the train. At the first station near Moscow an ambulance was waiting to take him to the hospital. Though stressful for everyone, the venture was successful. Zarubin got the necessary treatment and was soon back home. Four years later he died of a heart attack in 1972.

Fifteen years later Liza's life was tragically ended in an accident when her long coat caught in the wheels of a bus she was boarding. She was pulled under the wheels as the bus started moving forward. Her leg had to be amputated above the knee. She died in a hospital without the family knowing she was there. When she had not returned at the usual hour, they started a search for her by calling emergency hospitals and the morgue. They found her in the morgue. At the time Zoya and Peter, the son of Zarubin and Liza, were away on business, but they came back for the ninth day of mourning—the traditional sacramental mourning day for Russians.

Peter was born to Liza and Zarubin on October 24, 1932, while they were working in Europe. During his early years he stayed in Switzerland and was enrolled in a private boarding school while they were working on their assignments. He was three years of age before they brought him to Russia. He spoke only German and had to learn the language. Zoya often visited with Peter while his parents were at work so he could speak to her in German. She was his first tutor in the Russian language. Then he went to regular school where he excelled.

During adolescence Peter caught tuberculosis from a classmate with whom he shared a desk in school. Several classmates also had the disease. Peter's case was very bad, and Zarubin took him out of school for more than a year while he was undergoing serious treatment. He had special tutors, and when he recovered, his father urged him to play tennis and take long walks. Zarubin's philosophy was that sports could help heal. Later he surprised the family by becoming an enthusiastic mountain climber.

After receiving his *Cum Laude* graduation certificate he entered the Institute of Physics. When he concluded his studies at the Institute, he volunteered to go to the coldest place in the world, Vostok Station in Antarctica. He spent two tours in the cold region where his research was very successful. He was invited to the Ministry of Defense Industry to work on lasers. He became an outstanding laser engineer and was promoted in his department, eventually becoming a member of the Ministry Board. NASA later invited him to come to the United States in 1996. He also visited a research center in Great Britain in 1998. Now he is on pension and continues researching. He retains his professional ties with the United Kingdom, the U.S., and India.

Peter has a son and a daughter. His son, Michael, is a successful businessman; his daughter-in-law, Olga, is an English language teacher; and his grandson, Andrei, is a high school student. His daughter, Elizabeth, named for her grandmother, is now a homemaker taking care of her little daughter, Michelle. Shortly she will resume her studies; she is now going through the process of divorce and living with her parents.

CHAPTER 8

Professional Profile (Dean and Interpreter)

IN 1951 ZOYA ZARUBINA went to the Institute of Foreign Languages to apply for a position. She did not know how she would be received with the stigma of having a well known step-father in prison. She felt that she might not be well received, and she felt insecure because she did not have sufficient experience in teaching languages. But she loved young people so it was easy for her to get them interested in learning.

Varvara Pivovarova, the Rector of the Institute, was a staunch Communist and had worked for the Central Committee of the party during World War II. She was also a professor of economics. She hired Zoya who gladly joined the faculty. After she had taught for a while, the Rector asked her to come by the office. It was a nervous moment for her, but when she went to the office, the Rector told her that she was appointing her Dean of the English Language Department. She assured her that she had cleared it with the Party Committee.

Zoya was always patriotic and loyal to her country, but she did not feel the same about the bureaucratic functionaries. As a member of the party she had served as chairwoman of the Party Bureau of the Correspondence Department, and soon afterward she was elected to the Institute Party Bureau. In April, after Eitingon was released from prison the first time, she was elected secretary of the Party Committee of the Institute of Foreign Languages. The second time he was arrested she was relieved of her position as secretary of the party because she was "compromised politically." She did, however, retain her teaching position. She felt that the first time Eitingon was arrested, it was a tragedy. The second time it was like a bad dream.

Zoya held the position of Dean in the Institute for almost ten years and always had the very best relationship with her students. English was one of the biggest departments in the Institute with more than 1,000 students.

Since she had the trust of the Rector and the love and respect of her students, she was happy in her position. No one needed to know that she had to give private language lessons during her free time to meet the needs of her large family—each of whom was dependent upon her income and support.

When she was permitted to travel abroad again in 1955, she became involved in the peace activities of Friendship House which included the USSR-Great Britain Society. As Dean, she was a board member and went to Great Britain. When she returned hundreds of students would come to her lectures to hear the details of her visit: what the people were like; what the streets were like; and what was happening in Great Britain. They could not leave their country, but they gained global knowledge from her shared experience.

Through the years since that time, she has met many of her former students. Some are now professors and others high ranking officials. They all tell her that they remember the vivid stories she told them about her trips abroad and how it expanded their horizons.

She was still in demand as a sportswoman. The chair of Physical Culture would plead with her to participate in events because her name as a former champion would attract many participants and observers. She acquiesced, but it was an additional demand on her limited time. To her credit, she involved many of her students in sports, and they continued to participate.

Zoya received criticism from the faculty. They admitted that she was a good Dean, but was always lagging behind in writing her scientific papers. When she did hand one in, it would always be late. They knew neither her life story nor what the demands were when she got home at the end of her teaching day. They did not know about Eitingon's being in prison or that she was the bread winner for a large family. The Rector decided that only she and Zoya would share that information.

She had an excellent relationship with her students and defended those who were having a hard time. She particularly defended the Jewish faculty members in her department who were on the Party list for termination. When the Institute would reduce faculty, they would always have the Jews at the top of the list regardless of their professional qualifications.

Zoya was officially employed by the Moscow State Institute of Foreign Languages from 1951 until 1970. It was later renamed after Maurice Thorez, the General Secretary of the Communist Party of France who had been active in guerrilla warfare during the occupation. He had visited the Institute a number of times and, after his death, he was honored by having the Institute named for him.

Even though Zoya was employed by the Language Institute the Soviet officials could call her at any time for a special assignment. Such was the case when she had to go—sometimes for long periods—to the meetings of the Conference on Security and Cooperation in Europe. In 1961 she was approached by officials of the Ministry of Foreign Affairs and by the Minister of Higher Education. The Minister of Education knew her quite well for the work she had done in the Language Institute and recommended her to become the organizer and director of the first United Nations Language Training Center.

Translators and interpreters of English, Spanish, and French into Russian were much in demand. Those who had been doing the work were "White" Russian immigrants in the United States. They had, however, grown old and retired. It was not possible to find linguists for whom Russian was a native language. Most Soviet authorities at the time were not interested in holding such positions because they were more interested in important political positions. The Soviets who came to work at the United Nations did not know English. That meant many of the papers they worked with had to be translated. They would frequently bring them back to Moscow to be translated by Zoya's students.

An agreement was made that the Soviet Union would give 100,000 rubles and United Nations would give $100,000 to create the Language Training Center in Moscow and employ Zoya to be head of the Center. She belonged to a number of societies for which she volunteered in peace work, and when she traveled abroad, she would take a leave of absence from the Institute to take advantage of the time and do the extra work. Her pay ceased at the Institute and the Soviet officials would only permit her to receive $20 a day. Any amount over that had to be turned over to the Embassy. She worked for the United Nations Training Center from 1961 to 1970.

While she was at the United Nations in New York she decided to visit Washington, D.C. There she was invited to have lunch with Senator Margaret Chase Smith of Maine. After lunch the Senator asked her if she had seen the White House. She had not, so Smith said that she would take her over to see it. It was after visiting hours, but they could go in through the back door because the Senator had a pass. As they were walking through the hall, President Lyndon Johnson was walking toward them. Senator Smith introduced Zoya as a visitor from the Soviet Union. The President seemed surprised, but made small talk and moved on. Zoya said she had never seen such a tall man. Obviously he did not understand their presence in the White House, but was most pleasant about it. Later when she told Ambassador Dobrynin about meeting President Johnson and shaking hands with him, he told her not to wash her hand. Then he told her that she had been in Washington only one day and had met and shaken hands with the President while he had been waiting weeks to get an appointment.

From 1970 to the present she has worked for the Diplomatic Academy of the Ministry of Foreign Affairs. She began as a teacher of the English Language, but she did not feel that she was using all of her capabilities. Thus she moved to the Chair of Philosophy and Contemporary Ideological Problems. In this position she was able to share much that she had learned and was learning during the meetings of the Conference on Security and Cooperation in Europe.

She introduced new methods of teaching debating and public speaking, particularly on television and radio. After years of teaching languages she had become a confident and competent lecturer on world affairs and Soviet government. Her years of translating for world leaders meant that she had accumulated much knowledge. After hearing the debates she felt qualified to evaluate and interpret them.

In 1979 she came to the United States for six months as the general director of the Soviet Women's Exhibit which visited Baltimore, Chicago, Oklahoma City, and Seattle. The Soviet Women's Exhibit was an interesting experience. The Cold War, and the American attitudes it had fostered, influenced reactions to anything Soviet or Russian. As the general director she had to be endorsed by the Central Committee. She did not know who would be on the staff or how the program would be set up. Different organizations were involved in planning each phase of the exhibit and how it would be moved from city to city. These tasks were undertaken even though many of the individuals involved knew little or nothing about how things were done in the United States. Twenty-four people traveled with the exhibit, five of whom were men, including a representative from the KGB to make sure that no one defected or associated too much with Americans.

Zoya held frequent briefings to help her assistants know enough about America to make it, at the least, a good experience. They were receiving a minimum per diem allowance. Zoya and the manager decided to hold some of their money to be sure that they would eat properly. Otherwise, they were concerned that they would spend it all shopping for things to take home as gifts. The Russians are great gift givers, and material things were limited under the Soviet regime. In Baltimore and Oklahoma City, Zoya arranged hot luncheons for the staff to make sure they had a hot meal. In the other cities they lived in inexpensive hotels with rooms that had kitchens where they could prepare their own meals.

Among the participants were a doctor, a pianist, models from fashion houses in Moscow and Leningrad, representatives from the libraries, press correspondents, and the artists who painted the beautiful lacquer boxes while Americans watched. Everyone selected to go with the exhibit had party endorsement. Therefore, Zoya had to deal with people who were not necessarily the best at what they were attempting to do in the exhibit.

The Cold War seemed to be something Americans were very interested in, yet the blame seemed to be always on the Russians.

The commercial director selected the sites for the exhibit, and his choice turned out very badly in Baltimore. They were somewhere near the port and the red light district, so there were very few visitors in the opening days.

The announcement in the newspaper stated, "The Russians Are Coming" and none of the exhibit personnel knew what it meant. But Zoya had seen the movie and suggested that the other staff members go to see it so they could all laugh together. Things picked up, and more people came to the exhibit. Zoya was very happy when young people started coming from schools. Teachers brought their students so that they could see the people from that strange, far-away country which was "responsible" for the Cold War.

When the exhibit officially opened in Baltimore, Ambassador Dobrynin came to be with the group. Officials of the Soviet Central Committee sent the Deputy Minister of Culture to Baltimore to open the press conference. The woman's talk was the usual Soviet long bombastic speech. The official was very pleased with herself, but it literally killed interest in the press conference and the exhibit. Such a representative was to be sent to the opening in each of the four cities. After that first experience, however, Zoya managed to change the opening ceremony even though she was of lower rank than those making decisions in Moscow.

Zoya discovered that there was a large Ukrainian community in Chicago. Many of them came out to the exhibit and were eager to know how things were at home. It gave the staff an opportunity to speak Russian and hear more about the United States. They exchanged stories about World War II and seemed to be eager to hear any news or stories about their homeland. The Ukrainians gave a party for the group in Chicago, and they all enjoyed a touch of home. This connection helped the staff to get over some of their shyness. They were more willing to go out and distribute the literature and other information they had brought with them.

At this stop Zoya got a letter from a lesbian club asking if someone from the exhibit would come out and talk with them. She approached several members of her staff, but none would volunteer to go. For many people in the Soviet Union homosexual and lesbian are taboo words. Most Soviets did not even know what they meant and were even afraid to say the words, much less meet the people. Zoya went out and talked to them, and many of them came to the exhibit. It was a good experience for her and the staff to see this kind of freedom in a country. She was happy to make a number of new friends.

Another incident in Chicago is vivid in Zoya's memory. A distinguished gentleman, who was the director of the Museum of Science and Industry, called and said, "I challenge you to go to the Synagogue with me." Zoya responded, "Why do you challenge me?" He answered, "Because you are a Communist and you are not permitted to go." Zoya answered, "Who told you that we are not permitted? Of course, I will go." She went to the service and, while the service was in progress, negative remarks were made about the Soviet Union. Her host family was embarrassed, but later took her to a party. After they had a very pleasant time the hostess said, "You are such a nice woman, it is a pity that you are not a Jew." Zoya felt that they were surprised that she could be a Communist and a good human being.

In Oklahoma City they had another new experience. Many of the exhibit staff were permanent members of the Board of Trade in the Soviet Union, and their behavior as Communists was under scrutiny. They were invited to attend a United Methodist Church service. The staff said that they could not possibly go because they were Communists. Zoya said, "So am I but these good people have invited us and we will go." Zoya had visited churches on previous trips to the United States, and she knew that it could be a good experience. They went to the church and got a wonderful reception. Zoya always expressed gratitude to church members of all denominations for their kindness and help wherever she traveled during the Cold War.

Moscow sent another important official for the opening of the exhibit in Oklahoma City. This time it was the deputy mayor of the city of Leningrad (now St. Petersburg), Elena Yeliseeva. She was also an alternate member of the Central Committee of the Communist party. The exhibit coincided with Easter. Again they were invited to a church service. Elena said, "No, I can't go. I am a member of the Central Committee." Zoya took a risk and responded, "I am the boss here and I am also a Communist. We are going together because we are guests in this country and it is not polite to turn down an invitation when we are expecting them to come to our exhibit." They went to a big church where over a thousand people attended the Easter service. The pastor gave a wonderful sermon on peace and understanding. Zoya and Elena were treated like VIPs. They sat in special seats at the front and were recognized and introduced to the congregation. On their way out of the church many people greeted them, kissed them on the cheek, and thanked them for coming to the service. Elena was surprised that people thanked her for coming to meetings.

Later Zoya asked Elena how many churches were functioning in Leningrad. She said that there were many buildings, but only two functioning churches. Zoya ventured a response, "Don't you think that's not enough?" In spite of Zoya's remarks the two women later became very good friends. Since 1988, a historical year in church history, the Russian Orthodox Church and other denominations, have been active in many cities in the Soviet Union. It was a very limited number during the Communist years, but since the late eighties, all Russians are free to belong to churches and attend services as they choose.

In Oklahoma City the location of the exhibit was opposite the zoo. There were lots of children and few grown-ups. One day an elderly lady came in and said she had seen Zoya before. She had been in Moscow six times visiting the Friendship House when Zoya was doing volunteer work there. She was concerned that not enough people were coming to the exhibit and suggested that Zoya go to McDonald's with her. Zoya was puzzled and asked, "Why go to McDonald's?" She told Zoya that she would have a reporter there. The reporter came just as Zoya was taking a big bite of hamburger, and an item appeared on the front page of the paper the next morning with the headline, "The Russians Are Coming and Enjoying McDonald's." It attracted many visitors to the exhibit.

The models in the exhibit were beautiful; the dresses they wore were designer fashions. The furs were incredibly expensive and kept under guard at all times. The group was most grateful for American security. The security staff let them know that they did not agree with Soviet politics, but would do all they could to protect them. They appreciated their help and the sense of protection that it gave them. There had been threats of bombing, and occasionally there would be ugly shouts during the fashion show, particularly in Chicago.

In Seattle the exhibit had an excellent location near the Space

Needle. Zoya still feels very close to Washington state because it was there that she met James Talbot. He was the president of the Soviet-American Fishing Company, the first of the joint ventures with the Soviets. He asked her to come and visit the office. This contact resulted in another great friendship that was the basis for the first sister school relationship. Talbot was on the Board of Trustees for the Lakeside School in Seattle, and Zoya was the sponsor for a Moscow school specializing in the English language—School No. 20.

She gave him her address and telephone number in Moscow. Since this was definitely forbidden in Soviet relations with Americans, Talbot was not sure it would be correct to call her. But the next time he was in Moscow he called and Zoya answered. She asked where he was, and he told her he was downstairs. This was at the time when many older Soviet leaders were dying. Talbot's business trips seemed to coincide with the funeral services. He said that he had become a specialist in Soviet funerals. Each time he came Zoya would brief him on Soviet life and what was happening day by day.

An exchange of visits was worked out between the schools represented by Talbot and Zoya. Thus the sister schools had a good relationship and long term friendships were formed between the sponsors and visitors. The first contact between Russian students and American students was by telephone.

After the first exchange many friendships were made, and the new friends wanted to exchange letters. The mail service was very slow in the Soviet Union. It took six weeks for a letter from America to be delivered—if it arrived at all—so Talbot became an unofficial mail carrier. On his frequent trips he would have a suitcase full of letters from American students. He would return with the same suitcase filled with letters from the Soviet students who could not visit Seattle. The American students, however, could visit the Soviet Union. Now there are regular exchanges both ways.

When the Soviet exhibit closed at the end of six months, a woman from the State Department came to express her appreciation for the great exhibit, the lovely young models, and the videos showing outstanding treasures of the Soviet Union. At the end of her speech she said, "We know so much more about your country now and you have brought a secret weapon." Everyone was looking around in confusion. The State Department representative added with a smile, "This lady, Zoya, is your secret weapon." Zoya says that Anatoly Dobrynin has called her a "secret weapon" ever since.

After the exhibit closed Zoya was invited by the Press Club to speak to the wives of Congressmen about the women of the Soviet Union. When she arrived in Washington, D.C. she learned to her amazement that she would be introduced by Averell Harriman who had been the Ambassador to the Soviet Union and was at the Tehran Conference. When he met her, he remembered her from Tehran: "Oh, you are the little girl who was bossing us around at the Soviet Embassy in Tehran." Her talk was well received. She was ready to go home to the Soviet Union and see her family and friends.

Zoya had received a call from Valentina Tereshkova—the first woman in space—on her birthday, April 5, before she left Oklahoma City telling her that she was such a success, the Board of Trade had decided to send her and the exhibit to Canada for another six months if she would agree to do it. Her reply was that she was homesick and loved her country so much that she could not stay away too long. Zoya says, "I was worn out and my nerves were on edge." Valentina had chosen Zoya to be the director of the exhibit. She had also supervised the work Zoya did for Friendship House.

When Zoya got back to Moscow, Valentina addressed the Supreme Soviet and asked them to give Zoya a high award for the work she did to make the exhibit such a big success. They did not respond, but even to be considered was an honor. All-in-all it was a rich experience that the Soviet Women's Committee had provided for her. The Women's Committee was composed of executive women and, when Zoya returned from the United States with the exhibit, she was invited to become a member of the Committee. She had done some interpreting and translating for them through the years, but was not an official member. She remained a member until *glasnost* (openness) in 1989. Then everyone seemed to be concerned with problems at home.

"None of us had real freedom or privileges before *glasnost*, but now new problems have arisen, and these problems have made many women unhappy and frustrated," is Zoya's summation of the current situation.

CHAPTER 9

A Love Story

ZOYA FIRST MET BERNIE COOPER in Nuremberg, Germany, when he was serving as bench interpreter for the judges at the Nuremberg Trials. She was assigned to Nuremberg by Military Intelligence to interpret and coordinate the association between delegations. There was very little exchange between them in Nuremberg, but in 1955 she met him again at a sports gathering in Moscow. He had come back to his job as the sports commentator for Radio Moscow.

Bernie immigrated with his family and, as a Jew, he later learned that he was expected to keep "his place" in the Soviet society. He was not an extrovert and Zoya was, so he often observed her actions with surprise when they first started working together.

Their romance began when Zoya was thirty-six and well established in her pattern of life, but Bernie was understanding. When assignments as an interpreter took her to other countries, he would call or send her a letter every day. He always ended his letters with "love forever and ever and even after." He had retained some of the social habits he had acquired in Brooklyn, New York, during the first sixteen years of his life.

Bernie's grandfather had been a rabbi in Belorussia before the family immigrated to the United States. His father was a Soviet sympathizer—a Communist. The situation became very difficult for them as their activities became known. Zoya does not know whether the grandfather died in the United States or just chose to remain there. Bernie's father and mother brought him, their only child, to the Soviet Union because they thought there would be less prejudice. He had a difficult time because he spoke very little Russian so he went to the Institute of Foreign Languages where he felt more at ease. There he also became involved in track and field and basketball.

As an undergraduate he started working in the evenings for Radio Moscow. His father was working in Sevastopol as the head of Intourist. During the summer Bernie would go there to work as a guide for foreign tourists. He was having a hard time financially so he and several of his friends worked at night loading freight cars. They were young and enjoyed dancing, but not all of them could afford suits. They decided to buy one suit so they could go out one at a time. To make this arrangement work the suit had to have pants that would fit the tallest of them, a coat to fit the broadest, and they had to set a schedule as to which one would go on a given night.

After graduation Bernie was drafted into the army. His first experience in the mess hall was a disaster. When they brought in some fish and rice, Bernie said, "Oh, I don't eat fish." The sergeant came over and said, "You mean you don't eat fish?" Bernie responded, "No. I don't like it. Could I have something else?" "Of course," answered the sergeant and went over and picked up a plate of meat with baked potatoes. "Would you like this?" "Of course," answered Bernie and enjoyed the meal. The moment he was finished, the sergeant walked over to him and told him that he would be going on duty immediately. The sergeant took him to a large sack of potatoes, and he peeled potatoes until 5:30 A.M. He had to be on regular duty at 6 A.M. When the sergeant walked over to him and asked, "Who is it who doesn't like fish?" Bernie told him that he liked fish. He said that many times when he spoke out of turn, he was given special duties such as cleaning latrines, mopping floors, or any other kind of dirty work. Bernie had a lot of those duties until he learned that it was better to stay in line.

During the war Bernie joked that he was the oldest junior lieutenant in the country. He was transferred from one regiment to another and from one detachment to another. He chose not to make a career of the military.

Before the war Bernie was married and had a son. His in-laws lived in the Ukraine. His father-in-law was a miner and when the Germans rolled into their village, they were all standing by the fence watching. The Germans noticed a Jewish boy and snatched him and threw him under a tank. The grandfather resisted and fought them, but they tore the baby away from him. Later they threw him into a mine shaft along with other miners. It was a story many could tell about family members and their fate at the hands of the Germans.

When the war began Bernie's father was in Crimea. When it was occupied by the Germans he remained in one of the partisan detachments. His identity was not discovered until he was wounded, then betrayed by, a Crimean Tartar and executed on the square in Sevastapol. Bernie's mother had died before the war.

After the war Bernie was sent to the Nuremberg Trials. He returned after the trials with strained vocal cords from the hard work and many long hours of interpreting. He continued to have trouble with his throat and had to go to the hospital for surgery. One day, while lying in the hospital, the doctor came by and told him to get out of the hospital because he was faking it. He gathered his belongings and went by to see the doctor. The doctor told him to leave immediately and forget that he was ever there before it was too late. During the next two days all Jews of American origin who had worked at the Military Institute of Foreign Languages were arrested during the anti-Jewish drive of the Fifties. Bernie was saved by the good doctor who had spoken so abruptly to him and literally pushed him out the hospital while he was recuperating from surgery.

Bernie went back to his job at Radio Moscow as a sports reporter and remained there the rest of his life. This was how he met Zoya again. The British track and field team came to Moscow in September 1955. Zoya was on the National Olympic Committee. Bernie was covering the event for radio. When he asked her what she was doing these days, she responded that she was writing her dissertation. He was interested in her subject and said that he would be glad to help her. Although she later had to change her topic, she received a call from Radio Moscow asking her to interview for a job commenting on sports events. They would pay her well, and she needed the extra money to help support her large family. It would also mean that she would do the coverage for *Spartakiada* (National Olympic Games).

She went to the radio station and was interviewed by Bill Campbell, a colleague of Bernie Cooper. When the interview was over Bernie came into the room and told her that he would be the one covering *Spartakiada,* and they would be working together. Zoya was pleased with the arrangement. The romance had begun.

As they continued to work together their relationship changed from friends to lovers. It was a dream come true for Zoya. She had been working long hours to take care of the needs of her extended family. This left her with little time to think about her personal needs. She also realized that her daughter needed a father figure in her life. It was such a pleasure to know someone who understood her and her needs even though he was not related even remotely to anything she had done before. Together they covered volleyball, basketball, and track and field for Radio Moscow and had a lot of fun doing it. She could give up some of the private lessons she had been giving for a job she liked.

They were very happy together from 1956 until his death in 1975. Zoya says, "It was a wonderful time. I had something all my own. I had forgotten what it was like to be a woman and to be truly loved. He made me feel the importance of being feminine and being cared for. He showed me those little signs of appreciation, love, and adoration that I had never known. But the thing that really brought us together was our similar views on conditions and circumstances and the solution to some of the problems in our country."

Vladimir Posner worked with Bernie at Radio Moscow. Zoya and Bernie became close friends of Posner and his family. He has become a familiar figure on American television and has written a book about his experiences. His fluent English and extensive knowledge has made him very popular with both Americans and Russians. He now hosts his own television show in Moscow.

When Bernie came to live with her large family, Zoya's mother liked him very much. He helped the situation by complimenting her on her good meals. He talked about what was going on in the world through his radio experience. Mother enjoyed the conversations, and this relieved any tension that might have built up in such a crowded situation. Tanya, Zoya's daughter, loved him from the beginning, and he inspired her to study English. Zoya and Bernie would speak English when they were talking about things they didn't want Tanya to understand, but the time came when her grandmother reported that as soon as Zoya and Bernie would leave the house Tanya would run into the kitchen and say, "You know grandmother, I know what they were talking about." So secrets had to be discussed away from home.

Bernie wrote articles about sports in English for foreign newspapers. He would always sit down with Zoya and read them to her. She enjoyed this because it improved her English. Then Bernie started bringing interesting books, records, and tapes to which they listened. He would explain phrases or expressions she did not understand. Zoya felt that at last she had a well-balanced life, and a shoulder to cry on when she needed it. However, now she cannot remember ever crying except when she received the long overdue official notice of Eitingon's acquittal.

The only time they could be together without other members of the family around was when they went on vacations. They could not go to a hotel or *sanitoria* (government provided vacation places) and register because they were not legally married. They did not dare make it legal because of the danger to his position. The association with anyone who was a relative of a political prisoner could have tragic consequences. He also had the added problem of being separated, but not divorced, from his first wife. She took his relationship with Zoya as a matter of fact. Severe retaliation could come during that period on the slightest pretext which meant that everyone was placed in a position of trying to be understanding. Stella, his daughter, did not know for a long time who her father was with, but when she met Zoya, and visited with her, she was very happy about the relationship.

Zoya and Bernie would go on Black Sea cruises where they could ask for a cabin and not have to register by name. It was a time when they caught up on sleep. They had different time schedules at work. When they got home they would catch up on the day's events.

Bernie was working on an English conversation manual entitled, *A Course of Everyday English.* Later, when the book was finished, he brought it to Zoya pointing out the pages that Zoya should look at; they were about meeting a charming woman named Comrade Zarubina. He had included bits and pieces that would be good memories for them. In the inscription he wrote, "Books should be written about you not for you. Love forever and ever and even after." The letters he signed in such a way will keep their love alive and always close to her heart.

When Bernie was writing so much material in English for foreign radio stations, the Canadian Broadcasting Corporation asked that they have a direct broadcast with Radio Moscow. On the day the event was to take place the Soviet officials were standing at the glass partition when Bernie was preparing to broadcast in English with exchanges from Canada. Someone suggested that they make a bet about the first question that would be asked by the Canadians. They wrote their questions on a piece of paper and placed them in a bowl. When the broadcast was over Bernie had won the bottle of champagne for guessing that the first question would be, "What is the weather like in Moscow?" All of the officials were nervous about the possibility that the first and following questions would be ideological confrontations.

While Zoya was so busy providing for her large family, she became casual about her personal appearance. She was always clean and neat, but had no incentive to add the personal touches of special femininity. When she was planning a trip to the United States, she asked Bernie what she should bring him. This time she was not on her usual per diem as a Soviet delegate, but was being paid by the United Nations. He told her that he wanted her to buy herself some silk underwear. He insisted that it would be a gift for him because he wanted her to look beautiful. She realized that he really wanted her to look feminine and to care more about herself. The kind of underwear he was talking about was not available in the Soviet Union. It was then that she realized he wanted her to care more about her appearance. From then on, whenever she went shopping, she paid attention to how her dress reflected on her image.

Bernie's health was not good from the time he received a head injury in World War II. At that time he was shell-shocked and had lost his speech for several months. It was suggested to him that he should not work at a job that was too mentally stimulating. He ignored the suggestions because he loved his radio work. He knew it very well and felt needed. He had also become a confidant to many of the immigrants from the United States and other countries. Many who had serious problems would confide in him as he gave them moral support. He wanted to continue to be in a position to help them, as well as do his broadcasting. This was another tie that bound Bernie and Zoya as a devoted couple because she had been giving the same moral support to her friends and acquaintances. Life was hard for most people in the Soviet Union, especially immigrants, during that period. Any words of consolation from a confident person, especially a friend, were meaningful.

Some time after they were officially married they went on vacation to Riga, Latvia. By this time it was safe for Bernie because Zoya's step-father was out of prison, and Stalin was dead. While they were in Riga, Tanya came with her husband, and Bernie's daughter, Stella, came briefly to enjoy the vacation. Early one morning after Tanya and her husband returned to Moscow, Bernie suffered a stroke. Stella was able to stay with Zoya for a short time, then she returned. Had they been in Moscow their reputations would have entitled him to the best medical care. But they were not known in Riga where he was placed in a hospital near the city. Since health care was free for those in need, patients usually used connections with officials to get the best. This time, however, there was no choice. The ambulance came, and Zoya went with him. He couldn't speak and was half paralyzed. She was stroking him and speaking in English to him all of the time.

When they took him to the ward there were many very sick people, but not enough nurses and doctors to take care of them so Zoya stayed with him. He could not speak, yet she noticed that tears would be on his cheeks when he looked at her. They were there for forty-five days as she sat with him day and night. She took a vacation from work. The doctors assured her that he would improve, but added that this was not the best place where he could be treated. They suggested that she get him out of the ward and into a better hospital.

Zoya called her sister in Moscow hoping that she, as a doctor, would be able to advise her. When she had no suggestions Zoya called a long-time friend, Joseph, in Moscow who was well-known in Riga. He in turn called a high official in Riga. They immediately sent an ambulance which took Bernie to a hospital ranked as a

Kremlin hospital—the highest rank in the country. It was a hospital for the highest ranking officials in Latvia.

Living accommodations were very limited. Zoya had been staying at the first hospital which was a great distance from the better hospital. It meant that for an hour-and-a-half she had to take an electric train, transfer to a city bus, then walk for some distance to get to him. Then one day a woman in the cloak room approached her, saying she understood that she needed a temporary place to live and offered her a folding cot in her home. She stayed with this generous Latvian woman for four days. By that time her sister had located her friend in Riga. Zoya moved into the friend's communal apartment while she was away at her summer *dacha*. Repairs were being made to their two-room communal apartment so the room she moved into was empty, but they gave her a cot. There was a long corridor and six co-tenants, but Zoya, being near Bernie, was very happy there.

There were many letters from friends, and each day she would read them to Bernie. He seemed to respond. She had to appear upbeat all of the time to create a happy environment for him at the hospital. She couldn't eat there so she had to go out and eat what she could quickly find. As a result she began having liver problems. But by this time Bernie was beginning to improve. She began teaching him how to walk again. Then he started speaking, and the doctors said he was well enough to travel. They told him that they had done everything they could for him, but what had helped most was the care his wife had given him.

When they returned to Moscow, they met with the doctors in the Institute of Neurology where her sister worked. Their diagnosis was that it could again happen. He could choose to be a patient or he could resume working and see the doctors regularly. He chose to continue work, starting with political commentary. If he had tried to continue with sports, it would have meant going to the sports facilities. He did not feel well enough to travel back and forth. He continued to help Zoya with her public speaking skills.

In 1972 the Ministry of Foreign Affairs appointed Zoya to be the interpreter at the Conference on Security and Cooperation in Europe. She told them that she could not leave Bernie for long. They assured her that it would be no more than two or two and-a-half months. By that time they would have a permanent sitting body in Helsinki. They also told her that she would become the head of the languages services, and Bernie could go to Helsinki with her.

She asked Stella, his daughter, to come and live with her father while she was in Helsinki so that someone would always be with him. Zoya had what she calls "house help" to come in on a weekly basis to clean and cook.

The conference lasted much longer than expected, moving several times to and from different cities in Europe. Zoya was able to come home occasionally for three weeks at a time. When she was with the conference, Bernie would write to her every day and call her once a week. One day the women at the post office challenged him. "What are all these bills about?" He answered, "I am speaking to my wife." They countered, "Why do you have to spend so much money on her?" His answer was, "She deserves it."

Bernie called to tell her that she had a grandson and described him to her. Zoya and her daughter did not have a close relation at the time, but Bernie went to see the baby. He told Zoya all about him, including the fact that he was bald.

She was reminded of the time she told Bernie that she had always liked tall men, but did not like those who were balding and had a mustache. Since he was the opposite of all these requirements, he teased her by saying, "Well I would pass you by, too."

It was while she was in Geneva at a conference session that the word came of Bernie's death. She flew home to Moscow for the funeral having decided that the best thing to do was to go back and do the work that he wanted her to finish. Life had taught her that duty came first. The conference had moved back to Helsinki. Finland's President Kekkonen sent an invitation to her for the final reception, adding a personal condolence for the loss of her husband. Many of the international delegates and representatives told her how sorry they were about her loss. It helped to know that so many people were aware of her sorrow.

CHAPTER 10

Object—Peace in the World

THE PEOPLE IN THE Soviet Union went through difficult times. All countries have such periods now and then, but it seemed that the Soviet people were having difficulty all of the time—especially the continuing shortage of food and clothing. Through the thirties and fifties every family in the country suffered in one way or another. In the forties so many men were killed during the war, that those who were left became the treasures of society. Millions of ordinary citizens were killed during the war as well.

Zoya says, "We were dreamers and we remain dreamers. We felt strong and proud because we had the dream that everyone could be equal. We thought we were going to make it come true after World War II. Tragedy went hand in hand with the feeling of pride and happiness about our accomplishments. It was like the struggle going on now. Our wonderful dream of equality for all was too much for some as the going got tough. You can't force a dream upon all of the people. Some lost interest in work and had no incentive. Some became disillusioned, angry, depressed, and cynical. I am still a dreamer, and it hurts me that in such a short period of time so many things have changed for the worst.

"We know that on close scrutiny so much has changed for the better, but when people no longer have a dream, there is nothing to look forward to. Our people were forced into becoming pragmatic, and they are tired of struggling through each day making do. There was nothing wrong with Communism. It is the way the ideals have been warped and misused by the Communist Party leadership to the detriment of the Soviet people and the workers of the world."

Zoya became very interested in doing everything she could for peace in the world. "My interest in peace started way back in 1943; I was in Stalingrad two weeks after it was liberated, and I saw what it was like. It was one thing to hear about devastation, but quite another to witness the suffering and degradation. I saw the survivors trying to get back to a normal life, and all of those houses looked like skeletons glaring at you with nothing inside. People were trying to move back into their burned-out homes and get started with life again. I decided that the worst thing that can happen to people is war.

"This was the first time I had seen so many prisoners of war. It was winter, and they were thin and shabbily dressed, but for me they were still our enemies. They were being marched through the city. They had created the destruction in front of me and all over the city.

"Then on July 17, 1944, Stalin and his State Committee of Defense decided to have German prisoners of war march along the Garden Ring in Moscow. There were 57,000 of them. Some of the officers who were translators with those prisoners were my colleagues, and they told me that the Germans were scared out of their wits. They thought surely the people would tear them apart.

"They came from different parts of the country and were assembled at the race course. It was heavily guarded. Thousands of people crowded around the Garden Ring. Then came the ragged prisoners. That scene turned my life around. We already knew that the Germans would be defeated and that we would reach Berlin soon, but when I saw the first rows of Nazi officers with their polished boots marching in goose-step followed by tired, scared, and worn-out German soldiers, shuffling their feet from weariness, suddenly I had a strong feeling of compassion as I realized that they were someone's sons, brothers, and husbands. So the Stalingrad experience in 1943 and the Moscow march in 1944 made me feel that war is never just. For the first time I saw those prisoners as human beings who had acted under orders and were suffering for it.

"Many years later at the World's Conference of Women in Moscow (1987) we were talking about trust and discarding the enemy image. Some of the women said they did not trust my country. Dr. Helen Caldicott of Australia had organized Physicians for Peace, and she spoke about the role of physicians. When the question of trust came up, she asked me to respond.

"'Let me tell you why I am a peace activist. I was present as 57,000 German prisoners marched across Moscow in absolute silence, and my heart was torn at the sight. There were about 400 of us in the conference.' Suddenly somebody called out in the audience and came crying to the platform. A young lady embraced me and hung on my neck and said, 'My father was one of those prisoners. He told me that if ever I had a chance to go to the Soviet Union to say thank you to them in the name of us prisoners of war and thank their women for being kind and supportive while we were there.' He had added that when the prisoners were working, the women would pass them some bread and other food, and he would always remember it! I learned from that experience that if you have something to share you will always get a response that bonds understanding.

"Another thing that changed the goal of life for me was a reunion of the class of 1939 soon after the war ended. We were surprised to see how few of us were left. There had been the Soviet-Finnish War and the Great Patriotic War (World War II). We always called those classmates the 'eternally young' because of the age at which they died in battle. They missed their chance to contribute to the future of our country, to marry, and raise children, and be happy. We who were left were determined to tell the truth about our experiences, and help the young prevent another world war."

Late in the fifties she was asked to go to the USA, but her father objected because of the work he had done in Washington, D.C., as an intelligence officer. Even though she was going to participate in a conference on women's issues, he did not relent because he was concerned for her safety. There was still much speculation by intelligence officers in the United States about his role in getting the secrets of the Atomic Bomb papers to Moscow.

After the arrest of her step-father, Eitingon, in 1951 she could not get clearance to go abroad until 1955 when she received clearance to go with a group of scientists from Moscow University to India. She was nervous after being blacklisted so long and wanted to make sure that she did not make any mistakes. She also wanted to do a particularly good job because she knew that her friend, Elena, who was a KGB counter-intelligence officer, had recommended her for the assignment.

She went to India thinking that they all spoke Hindi, but when the Indian escort spoke English she realized that after independence from Great Britain it would naturally be the universal language. The group went first to Delhi where they were the guests of Mr. Nehru. Zoya had met him before when he had come to the Soviet Union with his daughter, Indira, and that was when Zoya met Svetlana Stalina for the first time.

After a few days they moved on to Agra where the Congress of Indian Scientists was to meet. Mr. Nehru had invited the scientists from Moscow University to join them. When they arrived in Agra there many people protesting and carrying black banners. Zoya asked the escort what it was all about. He told her that they were protesting against English as a national language, and they were speaking Bengali. Because of the disturbance the conference was canceled. Instead Mr. Nehru made plans for the Soviets to travel in India for a month. To Zoya it was an exotic trip. They lived in plush hotels which had been the palaces of the maharajahs, the former sovereign princes of India. They were served Indian tea. Zoya learned to love it. For the first time in her life she was living with luxury and creature comforts, and it was very special. They were doing a deluxe sight-seeing tour of India. They saw the Untouchables, the sacred cows, and were amazed at the terrible contrasts.

After a number of years Zoya was invited back to India as a member of the Soviet Peace Committee when the All India Peace Congress met in 1964. Zoya went as a delegate, but after they got to India she discovered that at the last minute they had canceled the interpreter. Once again she found that she not only was a delegate who was expected to participate, but that she would also be the interpreter for the Soviet group. The leader of the delegation, Professor Sergei Rumyantsev, knew only Russian. One in the group knew

Hindi, and another was a specialist in Urdu which was very helpful for the Congress.

The Congress was to be held in Cashmere in the northeastern part of India. In addition to the Soviet delegates, there were a senator from Italy, a diplomat from Delhi representing Cuba, and the minister of health from Czechoslovakia who gave the group some advice. He told them that they should get their delegates together every night before going to bed, and take a thimble full of alcohol because the food they were eating, and the manner in which it was prepared, was not safe for their stomachs.

When they reached their destination, there were 6,000 people waiting to hear about plans for peace. Many were undernourished, but they wanted to share what they had. They would extend their hand with a leaf on it. On the leaf would be something that did not really look appetizing. Zoya wore a coat with large pockets and would drop it in her pocket.

In the evenings they would go back to the hotel to exchange experiences about the peace movement. On one occasion they were invited by some of the Sikhs to visit in their homes. One of them asked Zoya if she had children. She told him that she had a daughter. He replied that he had a son, and he would be happy for them to marry each other. She was not sure how to react so she quickly talked about peace. Later she learned that his offer was a gesture of great respect and trust, and that he wished to be friendly and include her as a member of his family. So many of the people were like children; innocent and trusting. They tugged at the heart strings, but they were eager to hear anything the delegates were saying about peace in the world.

The delegation returned to Delhi. Some had returned to their country, but the remaining Italian, Cuban, Czechoslovakian, and four Soviet delegates were invited to meet with Mr. Nehru. This was arranged by a woman who was the editor of a popular Delhi newspaper and active in the World Peace Council.

When they arrived at his office, the desk was in the shape of a horse shoe, and his chair stood on a platform so that he sat higher than the guests. They were told not to shake his hand vigorously because he was not well and very weak. Being the only woman in the group, Zoya sat opposite Mr. Nehru. She commented on how fascinated she was with his beautiful face, and the fact that his eyes mesmerized her.

The group received a warm welcome. Mr. Nehru asked each of them to present themselves. As Zoya started to introduce herself, Mr. Nehru interrupted her saying, "I've heard that voice before, and you have a very good command of English." Zoya was surprised because it had been a number of years since she was in India interpreting for the Soviet scientists.

The Soviet Ambassador in Delhi heard about Nehru's recognition of Zoya so the diplomat invited the delegation to help celebrate the October Revolution the next day (November 7). He said that Zoya particularly must come and have a little chat with Mr. Nehru because he had taken particular notice of her the day before. Then the Ambassador told her that Mr. Nehru always came to the celebration because he liked the Central Asian cantaloupes which they had flown in especially for him. When Zoya visited with Mr. Nehru she reminded him that she had been in India in 1956 as interpreter for the group of Soviet scientists. He told her that he hoped she had enjoyed her visits to India.

Zoya was so impressed because she had read Nehru's *Memoirs.* Now she had visited with the man. When she returned to Moscow she told Bernie about her experience, and how great the man really was. A few days later Bernie called her from the radio station to tell her that the news had just come in that Nehru had died. She had visited with him just one week before.

The more Zoya traveled, the more she realized how much all people are all alike. The Friendship Societies expanded, and Zoya was involved from the beginning. It was an effort to have friendly contacts with other countries by having citizens and professionals come and be hosted by the Soviet Union. She was invited to join the USSR-Great Britain Society as a member of the board because of her position as dean of the English language department of the Institute of Foreign Languages. Later she was chairman of the Education Commission. This was when she started hosting many delegations of teachers and professors who came to the Soviet Union through contacts with the Friendship Society.

It was through this contact that she met Dr. Brian Holmes, professor at London University. This was in the late fifties. Once, when he was with a group of fifty-two teachers he went to a party at Zoya's apartment which was evidence of real thaw in attitude on the part of officials.

After their success in Great Britain they started working on a USSR-USA Society. All the Russian members of the Society had to be endorsed by the Central Committee, and they probably got clearance from the KGB. Zoya became a board member of the USSR-USA Society. She was also appointed to the Education Commission. "The Central Committee had to be sure how much they could trust us in contact with foreigners and how to check on our behavior when we were abroad. Mrs. Tamara Mamedova, who worked at the Nuremberg Trials and who, at the time, was a government administrator, became head of the American Department of Friendship Societies. Her father was a general, and her son is now deputy minister of Foreign Affairs. One day she called me into her office and told me she wanted me to be particularly caring to a new member of the Education Commission. I assured her that I would, and then she told me that Mrs. Nina Khrushchev would be the new member.

"She turned out to be a very pleasant woman—always punctual and participated in all of the meetings. She was timid and modest and never outspoken. The association with her extended my duties. She liked me, and when she had delegations visit her, she would always invite me to be her interpreter.

"She came to all the meetings when we were getting started with the USSR-USA Society, but before long she would come and whisper in my ear, 'You know, he himself is coming home. I have to go and take care of him.' That meant she had certain hours she had to be at home when Khrushchev was there.

"One day a delegation of the Women's Peace Walk wanted to visit with Mrs. Khrushchev. She gave them a good interview, and I interpreted for her. It was printed in a number of American newspapers. I met the mother of Bobby Fischer, the World Chess Champion, at this interview with Mrs. Khrushchev. She was a nurse and a peace worker who had come all the way from San Francisco.

"These women had come to talk with Soviet women, and this is how I got involved with many peace activists from the United States. Mrs. Khrushchev told me, 'I feel comfortable when you are interpreting for me. I don't feel that there is a go-between.' She added that things always went smoothly, and that she was going to recommend me to her husband.

"After some time passed, she told me, 'Don't think that I

didn't speak to him, but his response was that he would have no woman in this field and that's that!' So that was the end of her wish that I should interpret for him. However, I did interpret his speeches from the booth during large conferences—even his congratulatory greetings at the World Peace Conference. World leaders sent written greetings limited to thirty minutes. Zhivkov of Bulgaria, Fidel Castro of Cuba, and Sukarno of Indonesia sent written messages keeping within the allotted time, but Khrushchev was present and spoke two and a half hours, which was most embarrassing for the delegates."

In the late sixties Zoya started her trips to the United States as the director of the United Nations Language Training Center. Making contacts to help the peace movement was difficult because for many years the leaders of the Soviet Union did not permit members of delegations to give either a home address or telephone number to people in another country. They had to be contacted through official channels. But people found a way to meet because peace groups were organized in the United States which began to exchange delegations with the Soviet Union in the seventies. Because of her work with the Friendship Society, and her fluency in English, Zoya was involved in all of these groups.

Carol Pendell, California president of the International League of Peace and Freedom, organized exchange delegations with the Soviet Union. The wife of a United Methodist minister, she involved other United States clergymen in the exchange. As they worked with Zoya they all became lasting friends. In 1980 the Soviet delegation came to America for a continuation of the USSR-USA dialogue. Zoya was head of the delegation. For the first time there were many younger people in the group and also a Russian Orthodox priest.

When they arrived in Washington, D.C., there was to be a press conference, but as Zoya watched television at 2:00 A.M., the announcement was made that Indira Gandhi had been assassinated. The announcer suggested that there could be a Soviet Communist Party connection. Zoya knew and translated for her so she felt a personal loss. Not knowing how it would affect the group, she called Soviet Ambassador Dobrynin whom she knew well. He recommended that their press conference be canceled. That night the delegation went to a Halloween party at Georgetown University which was an unusual way to end their trip to the United States.

The Indira Gandhi report reminded Zoya of the story about Stalin's daughter, Svetlana Stalina, when she defected in 1966. Svetlana had received special permission from the government to bury her Indian husband in his homeland. Once there, she defected. The functionaries of the Central Committee summoned Zoya to translate and interpret for them because they had no language services. American newspapers and magazines were running the story every day. Their anti-Soviet attitude on this occasion was like that of their successors. The United States Embassy in New Delhi, India, had helped Svetlana get into the United States. The press was making much of the defection. Through translating the American media Zoya kept up with the story, and the Central Committee had to know what was being written.

Barbara Weidner, the Founder and Director of Grandmothers for Peace International, reminisces about the day in March 1987 when she sat with Zoya in her apartment and hatched the idea for the Grandmothers for Peace Walk in Moscow. Barbara returned to California and started to recruit participants for the peace walk. The day they were leaving the media was fascinated with the Grandmothers' optimism. The plan generated a lot of stories in the press for many reasons. First, the shock that Americans could join Soviet citizens on a peace walk, and secondly, that they were planning to stay in the homes of Soviet citizens. Both things were considered out of the question by the American press and most of the group's friends. In reality, they were expecting the group to come back telling them that it did not happen after all.

Television, radio, and newspaper reporters were at the airport to see the Sacramento delegation leave for Moscow. It was big news. When they landed for a stop in Helsinki, there was another surprise. Barbara had written to the grandmothers in Helsinki that the group would be there two hours between planes, and that it would be delightful if some of them could come to the airport and have a cup of tea with them. Upon arrival they were greeted by television, radio, and newspaper reporters. The members of the grandmothers' group and other women were holding up large signs saying "Welcome Grandmothers" and "Good Luck Peace Walk."

There was an equally amazing reception at the airport in Moscow with banners, cheers, and love. They were all overwhelmed. The welcome set the tone for the days that followed. The trip opened their eyes to the truth about a people they had been led to believe were not only enemies, but were totally different from that perception. Staying in the homes made a lasting impression. Americans expect so many creature comforts, and Soviets demand so little. But they make up for creature comforts with genuine, heartfelt hospitality. Barbara says that she will never forget staying with Zoya; having a "nightcap" before going to bed, looking out the kitchen window at the sights, and walking down the street as if they were two sisters out for a stroll.

Raisa Gorbachev could not be present during the visit, but sent a telegram to the peace walkers: "Mrs. Raisa Gorbachev wishes to convey to Barbara Wiedner that she remembers their encounter and the talks they had at the Moscow Forum, at the World Congress of Women (Moscow 1987). It is with great respect and sympathy she views Barbara Wiedner's activities and all the participants of the 'Grandmothers for Peace Movement.' What you are doing is very important indeed.

"Unfortunately, I do not have the possibility to meet with you, Barbara, and take part in the Peace March.

"I wish you and all the participants of the Peace March success and a fruitful and interesting stay in the Soviet Union."

When the group returned to California the press was waiting for them because of the reception this group had gotten in Moscow. It was hard to convince some people, but Zoya had set the stage. The people of her beloved country had expressed their hope and vision for the visitors. Peace is the great desire of their hearts. And once again Zoya's persuasive and organizational ability—well known to Soviet leadership—had prevailed for the peace movement.

In July of 1985 the United Nations World Congress of Women was held in Nairobi, Kenya. Rosemary Matson, co-director of "Continuing the Peace Dialogue," Patricia Schroeder (who works with her), and some of their fellow supporters were determined to go to the Congress. They booked inexpensive flights and registered for the Non Governmental Organization (NGO) gathering. Eleven of the group carried press credentials; they wanted to make sure that there was accurate coverage of these important meetings.

Rosemary had agreed to do a workshop. On arrival she discovered that it was scheduled for the first hour of the first day. She already knew that her co-leader would be Zoya Zarubina. Zoya was representing the Soviet Women's Committee. They had been planning this workshop, "The Role of Women in Adversary Countries in Transforming 'the Enemy' into 'Friend'" for more than a year. They wanted to demonstrate, by their cooperation in presenting the workshop, that women from different historical experiences and political systems could move beyond these differences. Thus, they could create peace through friendship.

Rosemary reported that the idea of women from the United States and the Soviet Union working together for peace was apparently intriguing because some 200 women crowded into the room at 9:00 A.M. There were some who had never before seen a Soviet. After three hours in the workshop, one Japanese woman reported to Rosemary that she felt more secure now that she knew women in the two superpower countries were talking to each other even if their male leaders were finding it difficult.

When Rosemary and her colleague, Patricia, had lunch after the workshop, they reminisced about the conference in Copenhagen in 1980 where the Decade for Women started. They agreed that the results of the workshop just finished were the fruit of the work that had been done during the past ten years. Their conclusion was that amid the perennial and frustrating battles being waged between nations, whether by military means or through rhetoric, there is a growing number of women who are choosing to move beyond these divisions to join hands across political and economic barriers in search of new solutions to old problems. Fences and borders are man-made and artificial. The future is in the hands and hearts of women.

A number of groups went to the Soviet Union (and later Russia) under Rosemary's sponsorship. Zoya worked with them, doing much of the interpreting. In 1994 an international conference was held in Alushta in Crimea. There were female representatives from America, Finland, Croatia, Germany, Serbia, Belorussia, and Russia. The discussions covered nuclear disarmament, women's health, social services, and the environment.

It was the first time that Tartar women had the opportunity to express their anger at having been placed in exile under Stalin. They were very vocal about all of the suffering they had experienced through the years by having been torn from their homes, then relocated in distant areas of the USSR, just as many other ethnic groups had been moved to less accessible areas. One woman, a medical doctor, remembered that she had been removed from her home in Crimea fifty years before at the age of four. She remembered the house her family lived in and grieved that her mother and father died never having been able to return to their home. She pointed out that they were not permitted to speak their own language, but had to learn Russian. She grieved that she could not teach her grandchildren any Tartar legends and songs because they had no books in the Tartar language.

Zoya says that now all of these groups want to return to their original homes, and that is the reason for so much unrest in the south of Russia. A good example is Chechnya where the ethnic residents want their homes back and are fighting for them. As the children and grandchildren come back to their original homes there is no place for them to live. The Europe National Congress reported that all of the deported nationalities and ethnic groups had been rehabilitated, but that is neither an honest nor a true report.

Stalin exiled many of the ethnic minorities to Central Asia, accusing them of high treason during the German occupation in World War II. When the government changed forty years later, they started coming back to their homes. At Alushta the Tartar women let it be known that they want to build again their ethnic culture. They want places to live and employment opportunities. They have to build new houses and start kindergartens. The central government did help, but Yeltsin froze the implementation until January 1997. Since then there has been war in the area.

The women from the Ukraine and Belorussia also expressed their heartbreak and disappointment about the way they had been treated under Stalin. They were angry that his decision was honored for forty years. Zoya expressed compassion for their suffering, assuring them that the rank-and-file citizens of the country felt the same way. The planners of the conference promised to do whatever they could to help these women who had suffered so much just because of their ethnicity.

The women who felt so helpless when they came to the conference were hugging and kissing Zoya and telling her that they felt they had won the first victory on the road to full reinstatement.

Zoya believed that much had been accomplished. She said that while men are waiting to open a dialogue with others, women can move ahead both intellectually and emotionally. It is only through giving people an opportunity to share what has been happening in their lives and listen while they pour out the feelings from their hearts, that people can begin to understand and know what to do to be supportive. The next step then is to have the courage to be supportive. Zarubina has this quality in abundance.

Dr. Ann Copple, a teacher of French, Spanish, and Russian in the Unified School District of Claremont, California, worked with the Claremont Association for Mutual American-Soviet Understanding. This is a group of women who wanted to work seriously toward a better understanding between the two countries. She worked with the USSR-USA Society and went with delegations to the Soviet Union. When a Soviet delegation came to Claremont, she asked Vitalina Koval to speak to a college group and to the women's association. Vitalina reported to the women's group when she returned to Moscow. They decided to start exchanges with the women of Claremont. Zoya worked with the group, thus becoming acquainted with Ann Copple. Later Ann spent a year teaching English in a Moscow college.

Ann first met Vita when she spoke at the Athenaeum in Claremont in the spring of 1988. After the speech, Ann spoke to her in Russian, telling her that she had been with the American group of teachers of Russian who had spent an hour with Gorbachev the previous August. Vita recognized her face in the audience because she had seen the hour long televised program with Gorbachev and the teachers in conversation.

Ann attended the Herzen Institute in St. Petersburg the following summer as an American Teacher Exchange Delegate and Rockefeller Fellow. Vita called and asked her to meet with her in Moscow when she was en route home. After this meeting the exchange conferences were set. The Moscow group came to Claremont in 1989 and 1991. The Claremont group went to Moscow in 1990 and 1993. Southern California participated enthusiastically in the conferences with even the media cooperating.

On Ann's first journey to Leningrad (St. Petersburg) in 1987 she read an editorial from the *St. Louis-Post Dispatch* while in flight. It was first published on October 7, 1984:

What is desperately needed is a clear break from the sort of xenophobia that causes Ronald Reagan to name Russia an evil empire. All creatures fear most that which they know least. Human beings are not free from this dictum. The only sure way to break down the barriers of distrust built up by both sides over the last 40 years is to trust. But we will not trust that which we have not allowed ourselves to know and understand.

Therefore, we need more, not fewer, cultural exchange programs with the Soviet Union. We need to issue more, not fewer visas to Soviet citizens. Our curricula, from primary school through to the university, must be examined with a critically naked eye—no longer wearing the rose-colored glasses of national security ideology. We need to teach our children Soviet literature and history, let them learn Soviet music and study Soviet geography.

For as Longfellow wrote, "If we could read the secret history of our enemies, we should find in each person's life, sorrow and suffering enough to disarm all hostility." Understanding of the other, based on sound knowledge, is the key that will open the disarmament door.

This is the philosophy upon which all the women's groups are based. As they work to teach and experience true internationalism, humanistic, and ethical values will change the way people of the world see each other.

Ann Copple met Zoya in May 1990 at the second conference of the women's groups. Ann reports that her effectiveness was immediately apparent both behind the scenes in "making things happen" and as a group leader capable of dealing diplomatically, but firmly, with occasional misunderstandings and disagreements. She impressed all of the women as a forceful speaker and a humane person with an engaging sense of humor. The rollicking "pot luck" dinner which was in Zoya's apartment is one of Ann's favorite memories. The Americans had brought packages of corn bread mix and canned hams. Ann says that somehow all of the guests (some twenty-five or more) seemed to fit around Zoya's dinner table.

In the fall of 1990, when Ann was on sabbatical leave to teach English in the USSR, she visited and spoke at Zoya's Foreign Service

Academy. In November Zoya took Ann to the Alushta conference where Ann co-chaired the education committee for the conference. Once again Ann marveled at the real extent of Zoya's talents. She was always able to coax, cajole, command, pull strings, and somehow get everything to turn out right. She was co-chairing the conference, interpreting, overseeing the final reports, and presiding over the final session with mastery, style, and brio. When the fourth conference between the American women from California and the Moscow Women's Dialogue took place in Moscow in April 1993, Zoya was once again the impresario who orchestrated everything to perfection. She was not the chair of the Moscow group, but she constantly drew on her wide acquaintances in International Educators for Peace and Understanding, the Diplomatic Academy, the diplomatic corps, and the universities for resources to supply the needs of the organizing committee.

In Ann's words, Zoya is unique because she is a universal person. Her wide experience of living abroad and of assimilating, then teaching, other cultures has made her perfectly at home wherever she is. She feels that their sensitivities are perfectly attuned even though Zoya's life has been so very different from her own. "It is her humanness which has made us all identify with her in the commonality of shared hopes and dreams for the future—of a world at peace. Working tirelessly for world peace is, indeed, Zoya's greatest contribution to her world."

In 1987 Michale Gabriel, an internationally known storyteller living in Washington state, traveled to the Soviet Union for her eighth visit, taking twenty-seven storytelling educators with her. The educators visited schools in Estonia, Ukraine, Khazakhstan, and the Soviet Union. They shared their storytelling and offered friendship to their Communist colleagues. They learned firsthand about life and education in their republics. Their experience of friendship and the information acquired was shared with American schools and communities when they returned home. They were convinced that the people of the two greatest nations should really get to know each other. To this end they made plans to have exchanges of educators between Washington state and the Soviet Union.

It was not that easy to set up plans for exchange, but Svetlana Pastukh, vice principal of School No. 119 in Odessa, told them about a new organization, International Educators for Peace, which was made up of members from each of the Soviet Republics. It had grown out of the Soviet Peace Committee with the intent of eventually becoming a totally independent organization. She told them that they would have to contact Zoya Zarubina who was the vice-president of the organization.

The first meeting resulted in an exchange agreement to take place in 1989. Soviet educators would travel to Washington state. Since that time Zarubina has worked unceasingly to foster the relationship between her organization and Accent on Understanding (as the American Group had come to be known). Zoya led the first delegation of Soviets. On this visit she impressed school administrators in Washington with her command of English, her knowledge of American ways, her ability to explain the progress of the Soviet Union in the twentieth century, and her understanding of the important role which schools must play in fostering this peaceful attitude.

Through the following years, Zoya worked with the delegations, and through her influence on the selection committee in Moscow, representatives from six different Soviet Republics participated as delegates. She planned two Peace Train journies for the group, taking them from city to city in the Soviet Union by train, and stopping for meetings in the various cities. Zoya's energy and determination have inspired the members of Accent on Understanding. She continues her work with the organization.

Chautauqua in New York state is well known for its interest in peace. Those who attend in the summer must be able to discuss both sides of all issues. During a lecture in the Hall of Philosophy touching on the relationship between the United States and the Soviet Union, Dr. Karl Menninger asked the group, "Why are we trying to destroy each other? Let's invite the Soviets here for a cup of tea and discuss it."

The idea grew. Working through the State Department, the invitation was extended. The Soviets accepted, and the first delegation of five people came to Chautauqua. The Department of Religion is the center of Chautauqua. Philosophical discussions are positive. The Soviets felt quite comfortable at the meetings even though before they came there was some apprehension. When the delegation returned to Moscow they extended an invitation for the participants at Chautauqua to come to Latvia.

The representatives from Chautauqua arrived in Latvia on two chartered planes. It was the first time that such a large group of Americans had arrived in the Soviet Union wanting to discuss human relations and to know the Soviets better. The Latvians were very excited. At the first meeting there were more than 500 people in the hall. There were two speakers for each subject on the agenda, one from the US and one from the Soviet Union. Their positions were quite different. When the time came for questions from the audience, the Latvians asked direct questions of the Soviet delegation about their own status and human rights. This had never happened before for fear of retaliation. Many Russians were fearful of the turn of events, but the Latvians were elated. Zoya, as vice president, represented the USSR-USA Society.

During the lunch break the Americans saw many people in the woods nearby who were prohibited from coming in to the meeting by Soviet security. Mr. John Wallace, international reporter for Hearst newspapers and a part of the Chautauqua group, gave an ultimatum: "If the authorities will not permit those people to come up to us and speak, in accordance with our agreement, we shall cancel the meeting."

In the evening the atmosphere was still tense when the TV space bridge between the United States and the Soviet Union began with Vladimir Posner and a U.S. representative as masters of ceremonies. An American woman called out, "You men should be ashamed of yourself; we have not come here to fight but to communicate. I am interested in knowing how to prepare Russian borscht!" That broke the ice, and the meetings continued as agreed.

The next exchange of visits took the representatives of Chautauqua to Tbilisi, Georgia. They were excited to be met by their hosts who held up signs at the airport, and were eager to take their guests into their homes. Many workshops were planned. Again Zoya conducted a workshop on "Women's Issues" while serving as the head interpreter. In the evenings there were concerts where both American and Georgian artists participated.

The Soviets came to Pittsburg for the next meeting with the Chautauqua group. The Soviets had a delegation of one hundred people from all walks of life. They received a hearty welcome. This time the Soviets stayed in private homes and enjoyed visiting the host families. Zoya conducted another workshop on "Women's

Issues." Hundreds of Americans came to participate in the workshops on diverse subjects. It was a most successful exchange.

The last joint meeting, as Zoya remembers, took place in Moscow during the time of *Perestroika*. This was the time to re-think attitudes and plan for the future. Much had been accomplished with the end of the cold war; it was time for a new beginning. People in the United States and the Soviet Union were learning much more about each other and the wishes of the common people through television and the press. Many realized how much the two countries had in common. John Wallace, the Hearst reporter, and Zoya were acclaimed as veterans of the meetings arising out of the initial dialogue in Chautauqua.

Zoya visited Australia and New Zealand in 1969 where she made new friends in a different environment. Her first visit was in 1969. Olga Chechetkina, vice-president of the Soviet Women's Committee and a well-known Pravda newspaper columnist, accompanied her. They were the first Soviets to visit Australia in many years. Freda Brown and Audrey McDonald, representing the Union of Australian Women, greeted them warmly. They visited many cities, and spoke at many gatherings about life in the Soviet Union and the position of Soviet women. It was their first experience of being able to stay in homes and enjoy Australian hospitality.

Freda Brown was the president of the Union of Australian Women. Zoya first met her in 1969. At the World Conference of Women in 1975 she was elected president of the World Federation of Democratic Women. Since that time Zoya and Freda had become close friends while meeting at different international women's conferences and during Freda's trips to the Soviet Union. It was a pleasure to work and interpret for her.

In 1990 the Australian women invited Zoya back to talk to both women's groups throughout the country and to Australian female parliamentarians. With much pride she told how things were changing under Gorbachev even though not all the changes were for the better. When Zoya returned home things seemed to be more complicated and disturbing. It took her a few years to adjust to the changes, but it still hurts her to see so many elderly women suffering and unable to cope with less material resources. Times are difficult, but she remains an optimist.

In April of 1993 a psychoanalyst named Vamik Volkan convened a therapeutic conference of Russians and Balts. Volkan had received a grant in 1988 from the Massey Foundation and founded the Center for the Study of Mind and Human Interaction at the University of Virginia. He began focusing on ethnic tensions in the Soviet Union. In the August 1993 edition of *The Atlantic*, Robert Cullen reported that, with additional grants from The Pew Charitable Trusts and the United States Institute of Peace, Volkan had started a series of sessions involving Russians and citizens of the three Baltic nations. Lithuania, Latvia, and Estonia had broken free from Soviet occupation in 1991. There has been little violence in the post-Soviet era in the Baltic states, but the possibility is ever present.

Latvia and Estonia have passed laws which have language and residency requirements that deny citizenship and the right to vote to hundreds of thousands of ethnic Russians, many of whom were born in the Baltic states. There is now a bare majority of Latvians in the country. Local officials want enough Russians to leave so that this majority will prevail in their own country.

The government recently announced plans to disinter Communist officials buried in a place of honor in Riga. Many of the remains are Russian. Volkan has found that few things so inflame ethnic tension as the disturbance of graves. He was prepared for tensions when his group met in April. The Russian government showed its support for Volkan's effort by sending official representatives to Latvia. Among them was Zoya Zarubina who had become the doyenne of the diplomatic corps. Volkan's group included two social scientists and three retired diplomats, including Harold Saunders who was a key participant in the 1978 Camp David negotiations between Israel and Egypt.

The Balts and the Russians both arrived emotionally conditioned to be defensive. They had grown up in a society where keeping one's true feelings hidden could mean the difference between survival or advancement. The Americans were asking them to let go of that defense so they could talk freely. It took a while, but they finally began to pour out some of their feelings. One man said that his experience had caused him to conclude that there were two kinds of Russians—the truly good and the truly violent. And during his life with them he had experienced both.

There were those who argued against trying to understand the

Russians. They had some rough things to say about their period of occupation. A young Russian diplomat spoke of the frustration and humiliation the Russians began to feel when the Soviet Union broke up in 1991. The Estonians made it very clear that they did not want Russians as citizens.

On the last day of the conference, Zoya suddenly remembered a conference in Rome in 1972. It was a conference of peace activists trying to find ways to end the war in Vietnam. Representatives of many countries were present. The Vietnamese had brought a news-reel to show the American bombing of Vietnam. To everyone's sur-prise the American delegates came to the showing. An elderly woman stood and apologized for her country's responsibility in the bombing of Vietnam, and she embraced the Vietnamese. As Zoya Zarubina thought of this incident, she had to speak and offer an apology. She said, "We thought we did a wonderful thing in 1939 and 1940 [the time when the Soviet Union forcibly annexed the Baltic states]. We thought we were liberating you from fascism. We did not know about the Molotov-Ribbentrop pact." *Glasnost* had opened up a new version of her own history for her. She continued, "I feel ashamed of what Russians did in Eastern Europe, not only in the Baltics. I apologize in the name of my family and myself."

Volkan was optimistic at the end of the conference. He planned the next conference for Estonia. It may be years before the effects of these meetings will be felt. It is hoped that they can man-age to avoid war in the interim. When people can talk to each other about their concerns, and be very frank about their feelings, it can change things. All too often, however, political leaders do not want to change.

The Diplomatic Academy knows Zoya's interest in doing any-thing she can to promote peace, and she represents them well in many international meetings. She also creates her own programs to work for peace in the world.

Conference on Security and Cooperation in Europe– Helsinki Accords, 1975

Z OYA WAS WELL ESTABLISHED at the Diplomatic Academy of the Ministry of Foreign Affairs by 1970. With a complete command of the English language, she was trusted and valuable to the Ministry. She credits movies with helping her get into the texture and rhythm of the language. While working in Intelligence in the 1940s, she had been asked to interpret foreign movies for officials who had to stay in the building until Stalin decided to go home— often in the wee hours of the morning. Foreign movies were only available to these officers so, as interpreter, it was a rare privilege to see American movies and translate them into Russian.

Before she began her work with the Diplomatic Academy she participated in peace organizations. It was a paradox that World War II had ended so many years before with no peace treaty.

Zoya was a logical choice to be an interpreter when it was decided in the early seventies that all European nations would select delegates to represent them in reaching a consensus about security and cooperation in Europe. All of the Foreign Affairs officials knew her, recognized her ability, and trusted her. She was a professor of

English and a lecturer on social and political issues. Her experience as a translator and peace activist made her a real asset at this period.

She was invited to join the International Secretariat's Pool in October 1972 to work as interpreter and translator for the new effort in search of peace and cooperation on the European Continent. After so many years had passed it was obvious to all of the countries that there had to be a valid plan acceptable to everyone, even though some of the countries had not been able to agree on anything since the end of World War II. For years before the Conference was finally called, efforts had been made by peace activists throughout the world, and especially in Europe, to bring the countries together. The need was growing for consensus in so many areas to avoid major conflict.

The ultimate agreements which might come out of the meetings in 1972 would not be a substitute for the peace treaty, but more of a working plan that would be acceptable to all after their representatives had forged a consensus. This unprecedented approach to negotiations began in November 1972 at Dipoli, Finland, not far from Helsinki.

Representatives of all European countries plus the United States and Canada were present at the first meeting. Participants, as well as staff members, were excited about the possibilities of making history. Each of the countries had two representatives present to sit at the table. Behind them sat the experts and counselors. The Soviets objected to having the United States and Canada as official members of the conference since they were not a part of Europe. The other Western countries pointed out, however, that they were allies in World War II, and the issues were about post-war Europe.

After President Nixon and Brezhnev reached agreement about holding a summit conference in Moscow on May 22 to 30, 1972, it was easier to plan the European Conference and hope for positive results. In Zoya's words, "The Russians are conditioned to put their best foot forward for themselves always." On May 31, the day after Nixon's departure from Moscow, a communiqué announced a positive advance in the relations between the United States and the Soviet Union. With all of the disagreement in the world, if the two top powers could reach agreement on a relationship and arms control, then delegates had a better chance of establishing security and cooperation in Europe. The positive outcome of the summit meeting meant a stronger foundation for cooperation in Europe.

After Nixon and Brezhnev met at the summit, and were able to announce that certain agreements had been reached, it opened up more opportunities for a better relationship. It also created an atmosphere in which the delegates could work to understand the conflicting attitudes and different social philosophies.

When the European Conference started in November, only sixty-eight chairs were at the table where the official representatives would sit. The Soviet Ambassador to Finland, Mr. Maltsev (as described by Zoya) was a typical product of her country. He was a former secretary of a party district committee and a typical party functionary. He decided that, as Ambassador, he was entitled to sit in one of the official chairs. But he was not an official delegate so he had to give up the chair. This was the beginning of frank and open discussion for which the Soviets were totally unprepared.

The first meeting at Dipoli started with an open agenda. There were no formal proposals on the table. A representative from Switzerland, Mr. Brynner, suggested that they call their proposals "baskets," and everyone could throw his or her proposal into the appropriate basket. This established some sense of order at the beginning. Out of the discussion three baskets evolved. The delegates could decide on names for the first two baskets, but it took a long time to choose a name for the third basket because it was the most controversial.

The first basket would be political relations. Its goal was to determine the foundation of the new political reality in Europe. What would be the cornerstone of political and official relations between member states? The object was to move the countries from cold war and confrontation to partnership and cooperation.

The second basket would deal with economic cooperation and trade. Zoya says this was important because it provided the groundwork for so many proposed projects. She tried to avoid working with this basket because she felt limited in her knowledge of economics.

The most controversial was the third basket. After extensive discussion, and much disagreement, it was finally named Humanitarian Issues. These were the problems with which the Soviets had the most trouble. They held out to the bitter end against approving it.

Zoya was particularly excited about the humanitarian issues which included freedom of movement, reunification of families, and freedom of the press. This last right included being allowed to go in and out of the countries with multiple visas so that reporters could openly write about what was happening in each country with no cover-ups. The final basket also included other humanitarian freedoms which had been and were taboo in Eastern Europe and the Soviet Union. During the Cold War in some of the countries sports participants were the only ones who could travel in large groups without interference.

This basket would also include free access to information about the cultures and education. It also standardized the assessment of certificates and diplomas between countries to make it fairer for specialists going from one country to another. Sports and tourism were discussed in the third basket. Again this area was highly controversial to Communist countries since they had functioned so long as closed societies.

For these intensive discussions Mr. Zorin, who was the former ambassador to the United Nations and a deputy minister of Foreign Affairs for the Soviets, represented his country. He insisted on knowing what was meant by a "family reunion" and further "what is a family?" It took weeks and weeks of discussion to finalize "what is a family?" It was not until after this discussion that the decision was made to name the third basket Humanitarian Issues. The greatest concern of the Soviets was the Jewish issue since being Jewish in the USSR was a nationality and was listed that way on their passports.

It became obvious that it would take many meetings before a consensus could be reached. Those meetings were scheduled at different times in Finland and Switzerland over a period of three years. They also had to discuss the subject of troops and armaments as well as the necessity of establishing confidence building measures on all sides. It was a major challenge because so much distrust existed on the continent.

The delegates and staff could go home for instructions and a bit of relaxation. Zoya's chances for relaxation were limited because she was expected to teach all of her classes at the Academy when she was in Moscow. She was happy to meet her students because she had new vocabulary and experiences to share with them. They eagerly awaited her return to class to hear about happenings at the meeting since they received practically no access to information through the media.

For the first time Zoya saw how unevenly the Soviets treated other countries. She realized that some of the American and British delegates wanted to cooperate with the Soviets. Since her feelings were already positive after her experience in Tehran, she wanted very much to be friends with the members from both countries. She was learning about negotiation and compromise, but was keenly aware that no one from her country had the skills for either. In all of their big conferences, the Soviet delegates spoke from the rostrum either appealing to emotion or denouncing the issues. Compromise was not a part of their agenda. Everyone listened to the leaders and accepted their proposals.

It was a momentous task to draft a document for the future of Europe, but the leaders knew that it had to be done. Staff members began to function as a unit. They had to be sure that every country would be ready to sign the final document. After two and-a-half years of discussion, bickering, and argument, to the surprise of all, the Soviets finally compromised on the humanitarian issues. It was hard to change old autocratic Soviet attitudes, but by June of 1975 Brezhnev tempered his position. The Soviet Union and Eastern Europe accepted all proposals because they were so eager to get the question of official borders settled. They quietly and officially thought that they could, at a later date, maneuver around some of the conditions in the third basket.

Zoya learned about so many things that shaped Europe and the world during those years. She still has very special feelings about the experience. It was the first time she had observed the intricacies and nuances of anti-Sovietism. As a peace activist she was able to see that the attitude of the representatives of her country was not always conducive to making decisions that would lead to compromise. She worked intently on the third basket. With her intense interest in the well-being of people, she had learned just how much those freedoms were needed in her country.

Professionals were brought in to clarify some of the most controversial issues. Their arguments forced all of the national delegates to think deeply about their reason for participating in the meeting. The delegates were made to realize just how much give and take there had to be before they could come to terms with the problems before them. As they became more willing to listen to others and share ideas, the pieces began to come together.

When President Gerald Ford came and spoke emphatically about working together, and hearing what all delegates were saying, he made the specific point that they could change things if they would listen to each other in order to evaluate the position of each country. At the break, many wanted his remarks in translation. Zoya, observing the process, remembered this to share with her students so they would understand how important differences could be amicably settled.

The Soviets had thought at the first meeting at Dipoli that the organization would become a new multi-national commission, but it took from October 1972 until August 1975 to get consensus. For many months they were not talking to each other, but rather at each other. Zoya, understanding the attitude of her country, knew that it was difficult for the delegates to conform to less dogmatic procedures. She could look at the issues objectively. The delegates from other countries often rebuked the Soviets for their unyielding attitude. These delegates were more committed to action that would improve the political atmosphere in Europe thus making it safer for everyone.

The Soviet Union wanted to dominate the humanitarian issues in the third basket. This was such a different experience for their delegates who had to have all of their decisions approved by their leaders. When the subject of private property came up, it was not something they could discuss because private property was unheard of in the USSR.

Often Soviet delegates would gain the floor and make long speeches—not always related to the subject. At one point Soviet Ambassador Mendelevich talked so long trying to show the whole world how good the Soviet Union was and how bad all the rest of the countries were, that when he was challenged by the representative from the Netherlands, he lost his cool. The Dutch official stated, "We did not come here, Mr. Ambassador, to hear you preach. We are all tired of it. We are looking for compromise—a way to cooperate—not to be your students. All of your remarks are counterproductive. Let's get down to business!"

Finally, when the long negative speeches stopped, serious work could begin. The decision was made that no borders would be y would remain as they existed at the end of World

t loyalty to her country, but she also wanted to help ys to cooperate. She was not happy with the long and eches being made by the delegates and officials from nion. She hoped that they would all understand that each consensus and that their behavior was not con-: goal. It was the custom to make very long speeches official meetings so it would be natural for them to ould follow the same pattern in an international con-elegate from any of the Communist countries dared hing their leaders said, but it was different with other

re thirty-five editors and translators who would put iments into six official languages: English, French, nan, Italian, and Spanish. All had to say exactly the ney all worked together on the wording of the docu-was the main language so Zoya was very much in was needed even more when questions would arise c versions had to be identical, and she knew English, h, and some German.

gn delegates would come up to her and show her a graph which they thought looked a bit strange, or it what they considered to be a scrambled expression. d if there were not a better way to express it in Soviets were so accustomed having to stay with the : the party that they wanted the document to read in osition. They did not realize that they were not the king Russian. They could not get by with having the n say anything that was not worded exactly the same d in other languages. They were not convinced, and would insist on their own wording which was very frustrating to Zoya, but theirs was the official word. She was in no position to oppose them.

When the editorial draft committee came together to endorse the text in all of the languages, the Dutch delegation said, "The English is correct, but the Russian is not." When the Soviets asked why not, the delegate from the Netherlands responded, "There are nine-ty-four inaccuracies and mistakes in the translation." They were not translation errors, but the Soviet delegates wanted the language to be vague so there would be loopholes for not honoring the commitment. This kind of response did not add to the respect for the Soviets, but Zoya felt better professionally because she had been right in telling them it had to be exactly like all of the other translations.

Zoya says, "Most of the time in my life I liked what I was doing. During the time of war, I did what I was ordered to do. You do not ask what is good or bad, you just take orders. I knew how very important it was for the wording to be the same in all six translations. You cannot do a little cheating and try to fool people. You are only fooling yourself and losing prestige for your country. But I was only a senior interpreter and could only give my delegates linguistic advice. The delegates were friendly with me, but I was seldom invited to their meetings.

"We did a lot of night jobs. Proposals would come in, and the Soviet interpreters would have to translate them into Russian overnight, and send them back to Moscow for approval, and wait for further instructions. Items in the third basket caused concern and tension. The ideological differences in the Communist countries were serious points with the other countries, but they all knew that the area of the humanities had to be settled before the final document could be accepted by all of the delegates. Many of the things being presented in the humanities were so new to the Soviets and to me that it took much consideration from Moscow before taking action.

"I was listening to the arguments on both sides, thinking about it, and writing pages and pages just for myself. There was new terminology and vocabulary, and when I would go back to Moscow, I would share with the students and faculty the pros and cons which surfaced in the discussions. I am sorry that I did not have time to publish a reference book on the terms used in the six languages, but I did lecture in a number of institutions in Moscow, and shared my experience with them because the vocabulary was quite new to us. I had to explain how it corresponded to the Russian. I labeled it a vocabulary of negotiations. It gave me an opportunity to talk to them about new ways to cooperate in a changing world."

To everyone's surprise, the Soviets suddenly decided to compromise. Later it was learned that it came about because of a discussion between Ford and Brezhnev. It was rumored that Ford said to Brezhnev, "Either we do it in July or not at all because I am running a campaign for President of the United States, and I will have no more time to debate this issue." Ford was filling the unexpired term of former President Nixon. For months everything in the third basket got a firm *Nyet* from the Communists because it meant changing their laws, and the way the leaders dealt with their people.

The Final Act was a blue print for the future of Europe. Zoya felt very much a participant in the making of this new world. Being a World War II veteran made her more aware of the necessity for a peaceful understanding between the countries.

When Zoya was first asked to take part in the CSCE (Conference on Security and Cooperation in Europe) in October 1972, she hesitated because her husband had had a stroke in July but agreed to go for a short time. She admits that they were naive for thinking that the Soviet Union was prepared to sit down at a round table with a new format and reach a decision on these major issues in a short time. After the first session Zoya knew that it would take a long time because it was so different from anything expected by the Soviets. After she became involved, and realized how long it could take to reach a consensus, she considered giving it up, but her husband encouraged her to continue with the challenge. Little did they realize that he would not live to see her complete this major project.

When the draft for the official document was approved in all six languages, the delegates and world leaders were called to meet in Finlandia Hall in July of 1975. It was a day for rejoicing. Zoya says, "This was not just another conference for me but a remarkable stage of my life. There I was standing at the top of the stairs, watching the world leaders as they were coming into Finlandia Hall; I was feeling so fortunate that in my lifetime I had been able to participate in so many important events that had shaped the future of Europe and the world. I was a young hostess at the Summit Conference in Tehran, and worked in Yalta and Potsdam, and here I was the senior interpreter for the Soviet delegation interpreting for thirty-five national leaders. It was a wonderful feeling of accomplishment. The younger interpreters around me could not understand why I was so elated—to them it was just another conference."

There was much discussion about the order in which the world leaders would speak. After discussing every scenario, it was finally decided that they would draw lots. This seemed to be the fairest way, and everyone agreed to the plan. When lots were drawn, it was the Holy See of Rome which drew the number one position. Zoya said that they accepted that as a blessing. The procedure worked so well it is now the standard in international conferences.

"I saw the president of France, Giscard d'Estaing; the president of the United States, Gerald Ford; Archbishop Markarius III; the president of Cypress; Ceaucescu of Romania; Brezhnev of the USSR; Helmut Schmidt of Germany; and President Kekkonen of Finland as they came into the conference. The Finns had done a wonderful job of planning the arrangements. It was well organized. In a way, this was for me the fruits of my modest contribution.

"During the meeting in Finlandia Hall, I interpreted the speeches of British Prime Minister Harold Wilson, Bishop Makarius, President Gerald Ford, and others who were delivering their speeches in English. When the time came for President Ford to speak, the secretary brought the text to my booth. On the top of the left-hand corner the words 'embargo before delivery' were written which means that this is not the final text—last minute changes can be made. I have always found it much easier to work without a text. Without the text you can sit in the booth with earphones and translate the speech as it is given without looking at the printed page and waiting for the changes that come while you are looking at the print."

When Zoya was to interpret President Ford's speech at the final meeting, she was given the text to follow word by word. All was going very well until she got to page four and it was missing! She said that it is an experience that strikes terror in the soul of an interpreter because one has to keep going while scrambling to find the page at the same time. After a few seconds she found it while she was continuing to interpret what he was saying into Russian, but those few seconds seemed like an eternity. The stress is indescribable. To add to the stress she knew she was working with internationally renowned interpreters who were aware of her dilemma. Probably each of them had had a similar experience or two in their careers.

After years of effort and confrontation, an acceptable agreement had been reached by all of the countries. The meeting in Finlandia Hall was a celebration which became known as the Helsinki Accords of 1975. It would be several years before the Organization of Security and Cooperation in Europe would become an operating reality. But after it became operational it has served well, with head-quarters in Paris, to settle disputes between European countries. However, at the time all of the delegates understood that no matter how well worded the final document might be, they would have to continue to meet periodically to review the need for implementation.

Zoya summarized, "I had worked at the General Assembly of the United Nations and at meetings in Geneva, and experienced the atmosphere of being in the presence of power, but what I experienced at the Conference on Security and Cooperation in Europe was a very real sense of accomplishment.

"I must speak of a negative aspect of my work at CSCE. We knew that our government had a limited amount of money to spend, but that could not justify the division between the delegates and technical staff. We were officially members of the international staff and were paid $120 a day as interpreters, but we had to take the money to the Embassy, give the check to the accountant, and get $20 back with the attitude that you should be happy to get $20. The delegates just joked about it. The state paid its percentage to the conference, and this was the system for seeing that we did not get more than our Soviet per diem. We were required to bring a Xerox copy of the check we received.

"Delegates often implied that the interpreters' jobs were the easy jobs. One said to me, 'Your job is such an easy job. When you finish you just turn off your microphone and forget all about it. We have to think.' What could you say? If they did not know how long it took to learn languages, and that the interpreters were the key to the entire conference, there was not much you could say to make them understand."

There were follow-up meetings after the conference. Zoya went to the one in Belgrade in 1977 for two months and to Madrid in 1980 for a few months. She then decided not to go any more because she felt that it was counterproductive. So many new people were coming in who had no orientation in what had gone on before. The arguments would be the same ones which had been heard in the beginning. There would be some very good new ideas, but it became too much of a repetition for Zoya.

She had a fortunate experience in Belgrade. She met Mrs. Margaret Thatcher for the first time. At the time she was the newly elected leader of the Conservative Party of Great Britain. Zoya says that, in her opinion, she is an outstanding speaker; poised, forceful, and always to the point as a leader and politician. In fact, she used videos of Thatcher's speeches as prime examples for her students.

While she was attending conference meetings in Switzerland at the beginning, she was able to hear the leaders of many countries on television. She decided to study their skill at getting a message across. She knew she could benefit professionally from learning as much as she could from the speeches she heard. She knew the languages, but realized that she could help the diplomats at the Academy if, while teaching them English, she could help them acquire additional skills in speech. She found that not many of them were interested. They thought that they were special as representatives of the Soviet Ministry of Foreign Affairs and could do things as they had always done them. These students also felt special because they were among the few who could travel and live abroad. But she continued to try. She believed that if, out of twenty students, three or four really tried and were interested, then it was a successful effort.

Zoya was an innovator as a teacher while other teachers were content to teach the old way. In her words, "It is too painful to change." Her advanced thinking has been recognized in some areas. Her studies have paid off: wherever she speaks, she is acclaimed as an outstanding speaker and thinker.

CHAPTER 12

Work and Rewards as Interpreter

ZOYA WAS BORN INTO an era and under circumstances in which her ability to learn languages rather quickly led her into avenues that placed her in top ranking services. When she was four years old living in Vladivostok their neighbor was a Russian engineer married to an American woman who spoke no Russian. She had a baby, but the infant became ill and died. She was distraught. Zoya's mother and father asked her to visit with the woman every day just to keep her company. Since she only spoke English, and Zoya had never heard the language, she was fascinated. So she kept going for the daily visits and, in addition to emotional ties, she learned some English words.

When she went to Peking with her mother and step-father, she attended the American school. This furthered her knowledge of English. Eitingon was later assigned to Turkey, and Zoya improved her skills at the British school. When she returned to the Soviet Union, her father helped to find a private tutor for her. He bought books in English so she could continue to read and study the language. Her love for the language continued to challenge her. She still has her first geography book which was given to her when she was eleven years old. She calls it a sweet memento because it opened the world to her. Even though she was young, she read it all in English and became a dreamer.

There were many people in the thirties in the Soviet Union whose language was not Russian, but most of them were put into concentration camps—some because they were aliens and others on any valid or invalid pretext. Languages were not taught in the schools so good translators were scarce.

Zoya says, "When you study language in your early years, it is rewarding for your future. It was probably destiny that my second husband would be an American."

She explains the role of interpreter and translator, "Written translation or interpretation, particularly in Russian, is not like oral speech. The structure of the language is different. So when we had the big party congresses and received thick copies of the reports of the general secretary of the Party or the chairman of the Council of Ministers, they were all diligently translated into bombastic high style written form, and when you started to interpret, you had to restructure the sentences in order to follow the speech. Those who do the written translation to other languages do not care how it sounds or how the interpreter had to catch up. They would put it in good style and turn phrases which made it difficult for the interpreter in the booth to do simultaneous interpretation while looking at the text and listening to the speaker.

"Translators write the sense of the speech into another language, but the interpretation does not always mean that you give one hundred percent of that on delivery. Some speakers are too fast, and some do not have distinct speech. You interpret what you hear and give the general sense of it.

"Some people believe they can interpret anything and everything. I don't think that is the right way to approach it. There is research which says that if you really go into the structure of the English language, more than sixty-four percent of all the words are what we call supplementary words. Articles, adverbs, adjectives, where, what, when, etc., are auxiliary. Some interpreters say, 'I know the language, I know the structure, so just give me the thirty-five percent of the terminology and I can do the interpretation.' But that is not the way to do it. Qualifications for a translator and for

an interpreter are different. In Russia, seldom is there a highly qualified translator who can do equally well as an interpreter.

"You cannot predict the focus of a speech, but you can predict
some of the words that will be building up to that focus. This helps
to keep up with the speaker. It is important to stay a bit behind the
speaker and have a chance to turn the phrases into proper language
either in Russian or English, or any other language.

"It is not expected, and often it is very bad, if you do word-for-
word interpretation. But you must get the feeling and mannerisms
of the speaker. The older generation of interpreters try to put themselves into the shoes of the speaker and bring the emotions across."

Zoya speaks from experience. For many years in the Soviet
Union there was no reason to have interpreters on the staff. In the
sixties, with changing times, the need arose. When there was a sudden demand for an interpreter, calls would be made to different
agencies and institutions where the best linguists worked, request-
ing that they be released from their jobs for a few days. Many of
those who could interpret were journalists, researchers, or professional translators of specified documents and materials such as scientific papers. It was not easy to get released from their jobs, but
with authoritarian state leadership there was no choice but to go
when called for a special job. They got very little pay, perhaps twenty rubles, for the whole day's work. These conferences could be for
a few hours or they could last for many days. Zoya recalls when the
Soviets were breaking up with the Chinese in the late sixties, that
one session alone lasted twenty-six hours. Those who were interpreting could not leave until the participants reached some kind of
agreement.

It has only been since *Perestroika,* in the mid eighties, that
more qualified interpreters and translators were needed to go to different countries with the Soviet leaders and important public figures. The Ministry of Foreign Affairs took the initiative by adding
a special interpretation and translation department. It worked very
well because everything was settled by contract. The interpreters
started being paid according to international practice—$120 a day.
If they worked more hours in the evenings, then they would be paid
a little more.

Before this special department, there was a World Peace Congress in Moscow. It was the responsibility of the Central Commit-

tee of the Communist Party to set up the language services. They would send a letter designating the persons they wanted as interpreters. Their employers did not dare refuse such important leaders. After all, they wanted to have good standing with the Central Committee. Zoya had to leave her job with the Diplomatic Academy to go on special assignment. In 1969 Zoya was called to interpret for the first Congress of Communist Parties. At this meeting the delegations made an analysis and assessment of world development in the sixties so they could map out goals for the seventies. At this time the Romanians were breaking away from the other countries. They brought 220 pages of amendments to the main document in small booklet form which was the beginning of their differences with the Communist movement. It was the first time Zoya had witnessed leniency and patience on the part of the Soviet Communist Party because they did not want to see the Romanian party divide the unity of the Communist movement.

Through the years Zoya has done much interpretation for public, volunteer, Academy of Sciences, and Central Committee organizations. It has all been done as extra work. None of these had a permanent staff until after *Perestroika*. When the Ministry of Foreign Affairs set up the initial department, it was an official association of mostly young people who could bargain with those who needed their services. Most of them were Zoya's former students and at times negotiated up to $200 a day and expenses if they had to go out of Moscow.

When Zoya was responsible for the interpretation and translation for the numerous congresses of the Communist Party, it had to be done in sixteen languages: English, French, German, Spanish, Italian, Arabic, Romanian, Czech, Polish, Bulgarian, Hungarian, Japanese, Vietnamese, Hindi, Korean, and Mongolian. The only place which had all the necessary equipment was the Palace of Congresses in the Kremlin. Most of the time they translated into English, French, German, and Spanish.

The Central Committee staff would choose translators for the written reports, call them from their regular jobs, and place them in *dachas* on the outskirts of Moscow long before the Congress began to translate the report of the General Secretary of the Party and the Five-Year Plan into six languages. This took about a month. As soon as the reports were delivered they distributed them to the press, then sent them to Soviet Embassies which distributed them in other countries. There were about 300 pages in each report. Zoya's job was to coordinate and moderate the oral interpretation when the Congress was in session. She also worked at press conferences.

Zoya sat at the keyboard in the monitoring room. In the Palace at the Kremlin from the floor of the big hall, one can see booths on each side of the four floors. The delegates were seated so that those on the right side of the platform would hear eight languages; those on the left, another eight languages. It was technically impossible, at the time, to get sixteen languages on the dial. The best and most reliable interpreters were pilots. If someone were speaking Italian the monitor would switch the speaker into the Italian booth where the pilot-interpreter would translate it into Russian. It would then go into the other fifteen languages from his booth. If this interpreter made a mistake it was multiplied by fifteen times!

The responsibility was a heavy one. Zoya felt it as she looked out over the audience of several thousand people from the different republics in native dress, wearing their medals and orders of distinction, and very eager to hear the speeches. The Communist Party Secretaries from the different countries sat on the platform as well as representatives from capitalist and third world countries. Zoya had the opportunity to accompany many of them and participate in roundtable discussions outside the Congress as an interpreter when they would visit plants and institutions, including the Academy of Sciences.

"At the Congresses there were always many subjects covered by the speakers, and interpreters had a hard time with specific terms. I would make lists of the specific terms in agriculture, industry, and economics in which I was not well versed, and put them in my lap while interpreting. When a farmer was called on to speak, I would quickly glance through the list of specific terms with their translations, and be alerted to the ones I would need in the rapid interpretation. Often the speakers would give a list of figures rapidly—that would be the hardest part.

"At the Party Congresses many speakers would report proudly about their achievements and use technical details which the interpreters had no idea how to translate. For the textile workers, chemical engineers, and chairmen of collective farms giving a lot of statistics, I would prepare myself in a unique way. I would refer to the Five-Year Plan where all the statistics and technical details were already translated, and write down on separate sheets making columns of special terms in different technical fields in Russian with English translation. As a farmer or engineer or economist came to the platform, I would grab the related sheet of terms.

Others began to do the same thing, and at the end of a session we would jump out of the booth tense and completely exhausted. And this was the job everyone thought was so easy! Either you have the knack of interpreting from a booth or you do not have it. Many who know languages very well have stage fright when they get into a booth and simply cannot do rapid interpretation. You must distance yourself from everything but the speaker and concentrate on what is being said. You cannot be distracted by listening to your own voice. If you begin to listen to yourself, you loose the thread of the speech. Some people can do it even though they do not know the language well. They seem to have the knack of ad lib and can carry it through.

"The thing that strikes horror in the soul of an interpreter is to be interpreting from a written speech and come to a page that is missing. If you do not have a written text you can ad lib. But when you have a missing page you have to listen as closely as possible to the speaker and carry on to the best of your ability until he gets to the next page."

Internationally renowned interpreters told Zoya that the World Health Organization had surveyed the physical and emotional pressures of different professions, and concluded that the work of the interpreter is as difficult and complex as any. It is not only the physical stress, but all mental functions are strained, making it so strenuous that frequent breaks are needed to recoup.

Zoya tells the story of interpreting a very long speech Brezhnev was making at a Congress. It was a written text which he had approved every word of before it was presented to the interpreters. The problem was that forms of expression in the written language are different from the oral. Sometimes what is heard in the Russian cannot be found in the English text. The translators had it in perfect English, but when listening to Brezhnev's Russian, it was hard to keep the place on the written translation because the structure of the languages is so different.

This time it was even more confusing because they were told

that Brezhnev was not feeling well so he would not give all of the speech, but would skip certain pages. There was a special building for the press called the Ministry of Foreign Affairs Press Center which had a large screen for the journalists to see and hear the speech. Because of Brezhnev's illness, the Central Committee cut out many pages. But when he started giving the speech, he began to read the pages which had been deleted. The interpreters were in utter confusion. Zoya was in the English booth. What he was saying was not on her pages. Suddenly a recess was called. After the intermission Brezhnev continued with his report for three and-a-half hours even though he was slurring his words and couldn't pronounce some of them. At times he really did not know what he was saying. To cover the obvious, the committee rushed copies of the speech to the journalists. As they came out of the press room they were given the copies in English. "One of the younger VIP members of the Party should have read the speech, but with us the iron-clad procedure had to be observed. We had to make believe that all was well."

At one of the World Conferences on Peace in Moscow, the schedule was well planned and rather tight on timing. Professor Bernall, the well-known British scientist, was president of the World Peace Council, and there were many distinguished people present from all over the world. Zoya was serving as the head interpreter. After she was briefed by one of the officials from the Central Committee, he handed her a schedule which designated that there would be a certain number of speakers in the morning; the afternoon speakers would be limited to thirty minutes each for their messages of greeting. Among those bringing messages were Sukarno of Indonesia, Madame Dolores Ibaruri from the Communist Party of Spain, and Fidel Castro of Cuba.

Khrushchev was the first to deliver his greetings. Just before he was to speak a messenger shoved the text into the interpreter's booth. It was eighty-four pages long. Zoya was shocked because this was a world conference; she had expected him to follow the schedule. Some of the interpreters were from the World Peace Council located in Helsinki, and some from other parts of the world. They did not understand why Khrushchev's greeting had to be so long. He gave an analysis of the world from the Soviet Communist Party's point of view. He was telling everyone what was wrong in other countries, particularly the "bad guys" in America, i.e. the capitalists. Zoya felt ashamed. She could give no justification for the breach of elementary rules of protocol and decency. Once again she was in a position of having no control.

The attitude of the Soviet leaders toward interpreters and translators was degrading. The Central Committee of the Communist Party and their escorts dined in a special place while the interpreters had to go to a bleak basement. Zoya's feeling was that the interpreters should be on an equal basis with the delegates and party functionaries, mingling and sharing meals with them. She finally had the courage to say how she felt because this treatment was only taking place in the Soviet groups. Change did not come quickly, but Zoya never missed an opportunity to emphasize protocol with her own delegates. As she worked in the Diplomatic Academy, she was able to speak often on the subject thereby helping some of those who were appointed to serve in other countries.

Zoya had interesting experiences in Great Britain as an interpreter. In 1961 the Soviet Union had its first national exhibition in Earl's Court in London. Zoya was invited to be the head translator. Her foreign travel passport was not processed in time so she came a day after the official opening. She was surprised to see that the visitors were staring at the badges which the guides proudly wore on their lapels. The badge read: "CCCP" which means in Russian the Union of Soviet Socialist Republics. "Why were they staring?" Zoya asked her British friend, who replied, "In Latin lettering it reads the Central Committee of the Communist Party." The first thing Zoya did the next day was to ask the guides to remove their badges; few of them were Communists, and they were certainly not members of the Central Committee.

During the month and a half of the exhibition, Zoya had a new experience as translator, guide, and administrator. One of her duties was to lead tours for visiting VIPs. One such person was the Red Dean of Canterbury. He was a very interesting, knowledgable, and kind person. He was well-known in the Soviet Union for his liberal views and interests in that country. It was a great privilege to visit with him. Later he visited the Soviet Union and requested Zoya as his interpreter during his travels in the country. This was a very rewarding assignment for her.

Also among the VIPs who visited the exhibit at Earl's Court

was the leader of the Labor Party, Harold Wilson. He took great interest in the detailed tour that Zoya gave him. After the tour the director of the exhibit, Mr. Borisov, invited Wilson and Zoya for a meal with traditional caviar and vodka. During the meal the conversation was animated and friendly. Mr. Borisov had to leave his guests, and asked Zoya to give them some Soviet souvenirs. Harold Wilson was sitting with a very young, attractive woman. When she presented the souvenir she said, "And this is for your daughter!" To which he retorted, "This is not my daughter, this is my secretary!" Much later Zoya learned the extent of her mistake when the man became Prime Minister, and it was disclosed that the young woman was much more than his secretary.

The most important event at the exhibition was the visit of the first cosmonaut, Yuri Gagarin. Recently returned from space, the Soviets had decided to send him on a public relations mission to boost interest in the Soviet Union and its national exhibit in London. As it happened Zoya flew on the same plane with him and saw what a rousing welcome he received, starting at Heathrow Airport. When his arrival was announced, hundreds of people rushed to see him.

He rode to Earl's Court in a red jaguar with the license plate "YG-1." Thousands crowded the sidewalks to welcome him. In the crowd Gagarin saw a small boy dressed in an orange cosmonaut suit. He stopped the car and let the boy ride with them. Many people took pictures, but the boy hid his face from them. When asked why he hid his face, he said that his sister spent the whole night making the outfit for him. They overslept and cut class so he was afraid that his teacher might recognize him. Everyone laughed. The young boy was very pleased when he was given special souvenirs.

Gagarin was taken straight to a press conference at the exhibition. There was a stampede. The British Press noted that not since the end of World War II had there been so many journalists present. Around 700 people crowded the hall to hear him speak. He conducted himself with dignity, and answered questions with a lot of humor. Gagarin was asked, "If Her Majesty the Queen would invite you for lunch, what would you say?" He answered, "I never in my life expected a queen to invite me to lunch, but if it happened, I would certainly accept."

The next day newspapers gave lengthy accounts of the press

conference, focusing on the invitation. In fact, at that moment there was no invitation. The detailed coverage of his visit made his popularity grow day by day. To the surprise of the Soviet Ambassador, Mr. Soldatov, the invitation was extended to Gagarin for lunch at Buckingham Palace. The Ambassador was well acquainted with the rigid protocol of the palace. He began coaching Gagarin on the details of royal protocol and the importance of table manners at Royal functions. Yuri said that it seemed to him that mastering these skills was more difficult than piloting the space ship.

When Gagarin and Mr. Soldatov entered Buckingham Palace, to their surprise, in the entrance hall they were met by 100 members of the personnel whom the Queen permitted to stand in the entrance to see the distinguished guests. Not knowing the set timetable, Yuri began shaking hands with all of them. The Ambassador looked at his watch in horror. They were a few minutes late for the lunch upstairs, but that was not all. Gagarin had learned which knife and fork to use during each course, but in placing his knife and fork on the plate, he dropped the fork, then bent underneath the table to pick it up. There was absolute silence, and he felt embarrassed.

After the ladies left, the men had their drinks and cigarettes. Prince Philip walked over to Yuri and, patting him on the back, said, "Don't take it to heart; it took me years to learn protocol. I admire your unsurpassed courage and daring. I was a pilot and know how difficult it is to fly a plane."

CHAPTER 13

Social Changes and Humanitarian Issues

RUSSIAN CHILDREN WERE brought up to be obedient, loyal citizens. Younger children were members of the Pioneers. When they reached thirteen or fourteen years of age they became members of Komsomol. Both organizations were planned by the Communist Party to start political education when children were young and impressionable, and the party could mold them into being loyal citizens. Usually more than ninety percent of adolescents became members. Zoya had to wait a year before becoming a member of Komsomol because her father was neither a worker nor a peasant. The Soviet Union emphasized that it was a country of workers.

Kids looked up to their Komsomol leaders. They saw nothing wrong with the system as they were being trained and conditioned to be good Communists. They were also being taught that it was their duty to report any criticism made by family members or friends about the leadership of the Party.

It was from 1934 to 1939 when Stalin began to round up people who were suspected, on the slightest pretense, of having negative thoughts about decisions being made. After arrest they were put into prison without a trial. Zoya, of course, knew many people who were being taken, especially her neighbors.

In 1929 the first Five-Year Plan began, and Stalin ordered that peasant labor be used for building factories and concert halls. Their overseers drove them so mercilessly that some peasants died while working on these projects after they were injured. They were compelled to keep working until they collapsed on the job.

Since Zoya's father and step-father were working in intelligence they were in and out of the Soviet Union while Zoya was in school. Citizens knew nothing of what was going on because the Communist leaders controlled all information, releasing only what they deemed necessary. What news they did let out, they couched in terms favorable to themselves. Since they controlled both *Pravda* (the leading Communist newspaper) and the national radio, only print and broadcast news approved by the party could be published. The people never had an opportunity to know what was really going on in their own neighborhoods. Even if they witnessed the secret police making arrests they could not talk about it for fear of retaliation.

Zoya graduated from high school with honors in 1939. She was busy with studies and sports, but in December the Soviets declared war against Finland to expand the territory north of St. Petersburg. Finland was always in the path of expansion.

All of the boys in Zoya's graduating class were of conscription age so they were immediately taken into the army when war was declared. It was her first close association with the death of people her own age. She was shocked when many of the young men in her graduating class were killed in action. It took a while to find out about the deaths because the government did not report to the families of the deceased. The word had to come back through men who were serving with them. It was a humiliating victory for the Soviets because so many were lost in action.

When Hitler came to power in Germany, it was Stalin's policy to cooperate with him all the way. Even though Hitler had explained in *Mein Kampf* what his plans were for the future of Europe and revealed his philosophy, it was not until Zoya saw the movie *Dr. Mamlock* in 1935 that she learned how the Jews had been treated in Germany. She was shocked again when she learned about the secret agreement between Ribbentrop and Molotov stating that the Soviet

Union would take over half of Poland and that the Germans would take over the other half. The Soviet half was divided up between the Ukraine and Belorussia. The Soviet people were told that it was a step to reunite the Slavs.

The second part of the agreement was that Soviet troops would go into the Baltics and overthrow the local government. This action would save them from Fascist power. The Soviet people did not know about this treaty. Those who talked about it at all were picked up and sent to Siberia. Everything was done without the knowledge of the people.

During the Cold War, and particularly in the sixties, the Voice of America began to come through radio channels. The Soviet people could listen in and know what was going on in and outside of their country. They were no longer put in prison for trying to find out about other countries. They carried their interest a bit too far, however, when the dissident movement started in the seventies. The Soviet leaders took action immediately by putting the leading dissidents in psychiatric hospitals and later in prison.

The freedom to know lasted a very short time. Zoya was brought up as a privileged citizen, but she felt the sting of friends forsaking her when her step-father, Eitingon, was arrested. The more she learned about the Soviet leaders and their decisions for the people, the more disillusioned she became. There was a period of time when she thought that she might be taken as they had taken her step-father. She did not speak of her tragedy, but she did all she could to shield her colleagues from injustices—many of whom were Jews. She led her own battle doing all she could to help them. Even her Institute director chided her, but she did not tell her to stop helping them.

There was never a thought in her mind of being disloyal to her country. Her parents raised her to be respectful and loyal to her country, but "not to Yeltsin. He is not my idea of what a leader of Russia should be. Regardless of what he says, he remains a party functionary in his mind and in his actions. He thinks he has to make all of the decisions for all of the people. It hurts when foreigners attack my country. Unfortunately, the people suffer now for having been brought up to be loyal—they deserve a better life. They never experienced democracy or individual rights, and they still do not know what human rights and democracy really mean."

During the Cold War the people were defending their socialist system. They felt that there was nothing wrong with it. They had guaranteed housing, inexpensive utilities, education, medical care, jobs, pensions, food, and cheap transportation—a true welfare state. Consumer goods were always limited, but they had the necessities.

An example of what can happen in a controlled society when young people have an opportunity to mingle with the youth of other countries occurred when the Soviets planned an international youth gathering. In the 1950s Soviet leaders organized a World Festival of Youth. For the first time thousands of young people came to Moscow from all over the world. The government was concerned about Soviet youth being contaminated with liberal ideas. Sexual activity got out of control, and the Soviet leaders did not know how to cope with the problem. An orphanage was opened in Moscow to take the children of Soviet girls who had become pregnant during the festival. Such negative information was kept from the people; no one ever knew how many girls and babies were involved. Because the festival took place in Moscow, the government built the orphanage in that city. The fate of either the children or the girls was never disclosed.

The Festival was such a colorful event that it was televised throughout all the republics. It was a first of its kind for the Soviet Union; more than 100 countries were represented, and many wore their native dress. It was exciting for all generations.

Zoya was then the Dean of the English Department, and about one hundred of her students were working during the festival as guides. She was very nervous when she heard that the police were raiding the bushes. If they found young people in the sex act, they would shave half the hair off their heads and send them 100 kilometers from Moscow as a temporary measure. Zoya never saw any students with offenders' shaved heads which let her know that no one was involved—or at least were not caught in the act.

During the first years of *Perestroika*, when Gorbachev was the leader of the country, the people experienced their first taste of freedom. After their initial feeling of elation, they felt frustrated, forlorn, disillusioned, and angry because previously the state had taken care of them. Now they had choices which they did not know how to handle. This freedom meant that they had to provide so much more for themselves.

Some people became rich overnight. This phenomenon caused hatred and jealousy among the majority because they were not able to cope. They were waiting for someone to tell them what to do as had been the policy through the years. They expected someone to tell them what to do to ensure that their needs were met.

Most of the people were dreamers. They thought that the end of the Cold War would not only bring understanding and reconciliation, but would turn the country into a democracy where they would not have to struggle for everything. When the dreamers realized that the West was not supplying all of their needs, and talked about it, the Communists taunted them by saying, "You thought that the West would take care of you. Now look where you are—you have nothing that you expected and it is getting worse." The Russians were always working toward a better society and a sense of individual well-being, but when the miracle did not happen, they blamed the failure on Gorbachev. The first time open elections were held forty percent of the people voted for Communist candidates believing that they could bring stability out of the chaos. They had forgotten the misery they experienced during Communist Party rule. People are intoxicated with the idea of freedom, but make mistakes in judgment when deciding what will be best for them.

Women continue to be the mainstay of society. They adjusted quickly to the new conditions (and subsequent unemployment) that had been non-existent during the Communist era. Even though many were well educated as engineers, lawyers, doctors, or scientists they took alternative jobs cooking, sewing, or clerking. In this way they could give moral support to their husbands and families. These jobs ensured that the family had enough money coming in to survive during the difficult time of change.

There were—and still are—many issues concerning women's health. Contraception and abortion head the list. About ten years ago six million abortions were performed annually in the Soviet Union. The deputy minister of health reported that approximately two and-a-half condoms a year were available to men. The abortion figures are still high—about four million a year. Women do not want to have more children because they do not know what the future will hold. Family life is hard enough now.

After the October Revolution the new government rounded up all of the prostitutes, and put them to work doing menial labor to build socialism. The reasoning was that prostitution was a product of capitalism; it should not be permitted to flourish in a socialist society. Many years later prostitutes would loiter around the hotels. The story was that the KGB had hired them to get secrets from foreigners, or to get a scandal started on designated targets.

The people seldom saw anything in the press about these stories. When *Perestroika* and *Glasnost* were announced in the late 80s, there were a number of interviews with prostitutes published in the press. Many of them stated that they would have never become involved if they had known how miserable life would be for them. In spite of the interviews, prostitution flourished.

There were several categories of prostitutes. In what was labeled the higher class, the women were well dressed, well educated, experienced, and expensive. This class caused a particular problem because men who were newly rich were using their services. They took the women on expensive trips to France, Spain, Hawaii, and other enticing vacation spots, eventually divorcing their wives. The first popular movie about the high class prostitutes, entitled *International Girls,* made the lifestyle appealing to young girls, many of whom wanted to follow the call.

A second class of girls practiced prostitution periodically for extra money when they wanted boots that might cost four months salary. They could make the needed amount in a few hours on the street.

The third category was most troublesome for those who cared about the women involved. These were the girls who came in from the provinces and would hang around the railroad stations in big cities. They were ready to serve anybody; first for adventure and then of necessity. The Women's Committee tried to talk with them, but they were hard to approach. After the borders were opened, criminals lured these young girls into going abroad to become entertainers in America, Thailand, Turkey, and other countries. Once they reached their destination their passports were taken away and they were sold into prostitution. Women's organizations in Russia are trying to help them but they can not get support.

By September of 1995 the police had identified 10,000 prostitutes in Moscow and another 10,000 serving in massage parlors, as call girls, or escorts. The situation makes it impossible to control social diseases with limited resources and no laws relating to the

Red Dean of Canterbury and wife with Zoya at the USSR Exhibition, London 1961.

UN Conference in Geneva, Zoya (in the booth third window); Deputy Minister of Foreign Affairs Borisov, Chair of Convention (seated at the far right).

25th Congress of the Communist Party, Nina Popova,
Chairman of Women's Committee and the Union of Soviet Friendship
Societies, Zoya as head interpreter.

Mayor of Rome and Cosmonaut #2 German Titov
with Zoya interpreting in French.

*Hall of Columns—World Conference in Defense of Children (Moscow)
(center front) Actress Stepanova (left front) editor of Soviet Women's
Magazine (right front) Central Committee Officer
and Zoya second row as interpreter.*

*Kremlin—leading interpreters of the Soviet Union for the 1969 World
Congress of Communist Parties, Zoya as head interpreter.*

Palace of Congresses—Zoya, head interpreter, with interpreters Victor Sukhodrev and A. Schweitzer.

Freda Brown, President of the International Federation of Democratic Women receiving the Lenin Peace Prize with Zoya as interpreter.

*At the Soviet Women's Committee during the 1981 Party Congress,
Valentina Tereshkova (speaking) to the left, Zoya and
Freda Brown of Australia.*

*Friendship House 1965, Zoya, Valentina Tereshkova,
and Galina Forlova.*

Zoya with U Thant at the UN Language Training Center in Moscow with Alexei Nesterenko, Assistant General Secretary on Disarmament.

Zoya and Secretary General U Thant at the UN Information Center in Moscow.

Zoya and U Thant at the UN Information Center in Moscow 1966.

(Front row) Mrs. Matlock, U.S. Ambassador's wife, Zoya standing behind her and Valentina Tereshkova (first woman in space), American and Soviet women having just given Valentina Woman of the Year Award.

Left: *Zoya's husband, Bernard Cooper (Bernie)*
Right: *Zoya and Bernie's wedding picture, June 4, 1967*

Zoya and Bernie's wedding reception

Left: *Zoya, Bernie, and Nicolai Kurnakov, sports commentator,
covering the National Olympics 1956.*
Right: *Bernie at the Black Sea during the honeymoon.*

Zoya and Bernie vacationing at a Sanatoria in Yalta.

San Antonio, Texas, 1984 USSR-US Dialogue greeting at the airport, Zoya, head of the Delegation, and a priest of the Russian Orthodox Church.

Zoya speaking to the World Congress of Women; Soviet-American Peace Dialogue Workshop.

Zoya and Rosemary Matson, 1985, Nairobi—first workshop.
Patricia Schroeder in dark glasses.

Zoya and Rosemary Matson in front of the peace tent given by
Genevieve Vaughan of Austin, Texas.

Nairobi July 1985 meeting of Soviet and American women with Zoya and Bella Abzug in the Peace Tent.

International Women's Seminar in Moscow—Zoya, Patricia Schroeder (California), Natalie Berezhnaya of the Soviet Women's Committee, and Rosemary Matson (California).

*Sister to Sister Seminar in Crimea. Zoya, Rosemary Matson,
Nina Tropacheva, and the conductor of the children's choir.*

*Sister to Sister Seminar in Crimea. Zoya, a U.S. minister,
and Tartar delegates.*

Barbara Weidner (California), director of
Grandmothers for Peace, and Zoya at Zoya's home.

"Accent on Understanding" of Washington State.
Zoya is received at an elementary school.

Freda Brown (right), Zoya and Nancy McDonald in Australia
with Australian Association of Women.

War veterans of the Diplomatic Academy
during the celebration of Victory Day, 1985.

Svetlana, Zoya, and Carol Pendell of California and
President of International League for Peace and Freedom
in the Park of Culture and Rest, Moscow, on Victory Day.

Zoya Zarubina
1995

problem. With the rise in prostitution came an overpowering influx of pornographic literature. Cheap translations are sold in stalls on the streets and are a large source of income for publishers. Many former political publishing houses are printing pornographic literature for high profit.

Homosexuality was another part of life that the Communist leaders had conditioned the people to believe did not exist. If they found anyone practicing it, he or she would be put in prison. For the first time in 1992 the gays and lesbians planned a conference to be held in Novosibersk movie theater in Moscow. They showed many movies and videos that were brought from abroad. It was an open house which anyone could attend. The interest of the media was aroused, and a number of correspondents were excited to report the new development in Russia to their home newspapers.

It was, however, premature for the rest of society. Many people expressed concern and described the activity as dirty and stupid. They believed that giving attention to those people should not be permitted. Yet the gays and lesbians attending the conference marched to the square opposite the home of the mayor of Moscow. They stood there kissing each other and distributing condoms. It was very distasteful to most people and morally unacceptable to older people. Nonetheless Soviet society was really opened to the realities of life during the first presidential elections in 1991 when a thirty-eight-year-old engineer registered as a candidate openly admitting that he was gay. Zoya says that now her people are gradually opening up to the realities of life.

Tatyana, Zoya's daughter, got an assignment from a British women's magazine to write about AIDS and HIV. She had a long interview with a gentleman who told her all of the good things that had come out of the gay-lesbian conference in Moscow. He stated that they should have their own publication because it would help to raise the funds needed to treat those who were in hospitals with HIV. Then he told her that he had AIDS. He added that a fund had been started, and the victims were getting money from their Swedish friends and gifts from Finland. Now they have their own network to determine who needs emergency assistance. Zoya's response is: "I think that it is a healthy development. I am sure that it will be some time before we can talk about it as openly as you do here in the United States."

In 1990, for the first time, parents of teenagers were invited to their schools for a briefing on drug addiction about which the parents knew nothing. AIDS was also discussed. A young man from the medical services gave the briefing where Zoya's grandson was in school. It was the first time that many parents had heard anything about gays—they did not even know the word.

Pensions are granted to men and women after retirement when women are fifty-five and men are sixty. There are now over thirty-five million pensioners in the country; more than one and-a-half million of them live in Moscow. Pensions were never large, but they did cover living expenses. Now the recompense is neither adequate nor received regularly. Today's minimum pension is equivalent to about $15 making it very difficult to survive. Utilities are zooming up in cost, and pensioners have to pay telephone and electric bills. Many do not pay their rent because there are no regulations about eviction.

Pensioners have been in a survival mode since 1992. Their diet is meager. For eight years they have not been able to buy winter clothes, and the ones they have been wearing are threadbare. No one dares to ask or think, "What is next!"

Since Gorbachev, urbanites have had vegetable gardens outside the city. They have a small plot where they grow potatoes, cabbage, carrots, and beets. One in every three have *dachas* which can be small log huts or even a heavy carton which becomes home during the growing season. Some also raise pigs, chickens, and ducks. This helps them get through the winter. They only have to buy bread, milk, a little butter, and cereal.

The new government of Prime Minister Primakov promises to allot more money for taking care of the needy. For the first time the big cities are starting soup kitchens sponsored by private enterprises, the church, and other volunteer organizations.

In all the years of Communist Party rule, children were the privileged class. Up to eighty-seven percent of the women were working or studying so the state supported a well-organized kindergarten system. The hours were from 8:00 A.M. until 6:00 P.M., and some schools had the children boarding for the whole week with parents picking them up on the weekend. Most kindergartens were either state or locally subsidized by trade unions. In June, July, and August the children could stay in *dachas* where the parents could visit.

Health care for pregnant women, child care, and maternity homes were all free. Prenatal and postnatal care was all paid for, and the woman's job was guaranteed if she came back within a year. Women doing physical labor were taken off the job to do clerical work after the fourth month of pregnancy.

Since 1992 families receive a monthly allowance until the child is fourteen. All medical care of children and families is still free, but they must supply most of their own food if they are in the hospital. It is kept in refrigerators in the halls of hospitals. The hospitals and polyclinics for party VIP's were very different. Patients had good daily rations, including fruit. They could also obtain all necessary medicines. Since health care is no longer subsidized by the state, it is practically impossible for most people to purchase what they need. There is a minimal required list of medicines that pensioners can get at reduced prices, but it is not always available. Today there are hospital and polyclinic services for the newly rich which can run from $100 to $300 a day where service is better and medication is available. This is the usual situation in countries where there are those who have and those who have not. Pharmacies have both a wide variety and large stock of medicine, but prices make these remedies unaffordable to most people. For instance, even a natural product such as Dandelion Root Jell is $19 in Moscow and $5.50 in the United States.

The school system in Russia now has 60,000 schools and one and-a-half million teachers who are teaching in thirty-six native languages, plus Russian, English, French, or German as a second language. Since 1992 one percent of the schools are independent. At these institutions parents pay from $100 to $300 a month per child, but these schools are still experimental.

Under the Communist system school programs were the same across the country. Now there are 100 different school curricula including computers, journalism, environment, and the usual subjects of classical education.

In these different programs, the teachers have free choice of the books they will use. But teachers are not satisfied with their pay and it is always late so there are strikes against the government—an unheard of possibility before the nineties.

Principals now can choose what their state allotted money will be spent for, and in addition they can rent their gymnasiums, swimming pools, auditoriums, or sports grounds to outsiders. The schools then use the money where it is most needed. For instance, they can use the income either to reward the best teachers or help them in case of long term illness.

Schools always have a shortage of teachers. Teachers of languages leave in larger numbers because they can get more than five times their salary by joining companies that need translators. This situation is also true of science teachers who are needed in private business.

In a population of more than 240 million only nineteen million were designated to become members of the Communist Party. Many who were accepted into the party after the seventies cared neither about the philosophy nor their involvement in it, but they wanted to be sure that they could advance in their careers which were controlled by party leaders.

After 1992 the Pioneer and Komsomol organizations were dissolved, resulting in a noticeable decline in discipline. Teachers complain of having difficulty in managing classes. This is alarming to women's and teachers' organizations. The latest data indicate that more than two million children do not attend school regularly. There are more homeless children today than after the Civil War of the 1920s; a matter of deep concern to working parent and volunteer organizations.

The changes in education are reflected in the changes in the country. Before the nineties there were more than 900 universities throughout the country. They were a symbol of prestige for the city or republic in which they were located. After students graduated they were obligated to work for two years in an assigned job to repay the government for their education. The state planned ahead for five years in each field to guarantee a job for each student. Now the number of universities has been reduced, and the state no longer guarantees a job. Education is still free, but the students must find their own jobs. This creates real problems because, with no planned jobs, graduates must seek and compete for the available jobs.

Many universities are offering only bachelor's and master's degrees. Students and teachers do not agree with this plan because they feel that it diminishes their chances for employment. Previously, students attended classes five to six years to get a complete university education, including medical degrees.

There is no longer money for research. Five percent of the enrollment can now be on a commercial basis. The cost runs from $300 to $600 for each semester. All entering students must take examinations. The ratings are excellent, good, satisfactory, and poor. Those making excellent or good grades receive free education. Those paying must get at least a satisfactory rating.

Of late students are more dissatisfied. Now that they are free to protest, they take advantage of it. There are many more mass marches of students demanding better education and increased stipends. The government of the regions react, but there is little they can do because they do not have the money to do more than they are doing.

Since the end of World War II there has been a system of orphanages in the country. First they were the children of deceased parents. Now parents literally dump their children. Some are sick and some have physical handicaps. Previously, people in general never heard anything about orphanages. They did not know the conditions in which the children lived. Now many, including Zoya, are shocked at the miserable circumstances these children suffer through every day of their lives. No one seems to be interested in improving the situation. An article in *The Christian Science Monitor*, January 12, 1999, describes the conditions in an orphanage in Dimitrov, Russia. A kitchen worker said to the reporter that she thanked God for their own garden which makes it possible to serve a small portion of a few needed foods. The orphans are disabled, and they have not had meat, fresh fruit, milk, or eggs in months. None of the staff have been paid since October 1998. Human Rights Watch issues regular reports that show there is a vast chain of Russian orphanages. The results of their year-long investigation allege that Russia's 200,000 institutionalized orphans are subjected to systematic "cruelty and neglect" and are deprived of their most basic human needs.

Russian experts say that the abuses cited in the Human Rights report are the exception rather than the rule, but admit that the system is not working. The director of Children's House 19 in Moscow explained that in today's harsh economy parents are simply dumping their children on the state. This orphanage is a clean and apparently well-run facility in downtown Moscow. Even though the budgets are tight, with the relative prosperity in the capital, this orphanage still receives its monthly funding of 1,000 rubles (about $75) per child—an amount close to the average monthly wage. More than half of the children who come to this orphanage have parents somewhere. The numbers increase every year and overburden the system. Approximately 15,000 young adults are released from orphanages every year. Of these 5,000 are homeless within six months; 3,000 are in prison; and 1,500 have committed suicide.

For the first time Children's House 19 has been involved in an experiment in which outside families are paid 1,500 rubles per month to take over a child's full-time care. About half of the home's children have been placed in foster care. Often the professional foster parents are unemployed women who can give the children some kind of normal life. It has become more difficult for Americans to adopt because of political posturing by the members of the *Duma* (lower house of parliament). Their stance is, "How can we sell our citizens to Americans?"

For years the Russians were known for their close-knit family relationships. It was the responsibility of the clan to see that children in need had care and Komsomol and the trade unions, when they were alerted to problems with the children, would work with the parents.

Orphanages were always hidden. Now, in addition to the fact that the people know about them, it has been revealed that there were over three million handicapped people in Russia who were seldom seen in public places.

In 1977 I was traveling with an education seminar group, and we were to take the overnight train from Tallin, Estonia, to Moscow. My seventeen-year-old grandson, Bob, was traveling with me and was a great help in many ways. Most of all he was resourceful and not easily intimidated. He spoke enough Russian to be understood. There were two retired teachers in the group who had difficulty walking distances. When our car was pointed out to us, the two women looked hopeless because it was a long distance down the track. Bob immediately went to two men in uniform who obviously worked at the station and asked them about a wheel chair. In disgust they responded *"Nyet!"* and indicated that people who could not walk should stay at home. Bob turned around and saw a nearby hand cart. He went over and pushed it to the women, and gently lifted each of them up and sat them on the edge of the cart. Once he had lifted each of them down by the train, they boarded. When he returned the cart, the men were still standing there looking stunned.

Although thirty-eight to forty percent of the population in Russia live below the poverty line, a recent poll indicated that the rest are just making ends meet. A poll taken in 1998 showed that only ten percent of the population is satisfied with the way things are being done.

After August 1998 the financial crash came. Now everything is worse. The fiscal disaster practically destroyed the emerging middle class, and without them there is no stabilizing possibility. People are angry and disruptive. They cannot foresee a future that is any better.

Nationalism has become a dangerous concept for both Russians and the peoples of the former Soviet States. Changes have come at such a rapid pace that many of the former republics want to blame all of their problems on the Kremlin and Russia. After the demise of the Soviet Union there are more than twenty-five million ethnic Russians living in other now independent republics. This will create a big problem in 1999 during the parliamentary elections. Russians living in former republics of the USSR are not happy because they are treated as outsiders even though they may have been born where they are living.

Nationalism also interferes with any attempt to unify the society in these trying years of change. Zoya has witnessed, to her dismay, the police stopping people on the streets of Moscow to check their identification papers because their features are not Russian. Mr. Owens, a friend of Zoya's from North Wales, was recently visiting in Moscow where he was stopped in the underground and asked for identification.

In spite of the difficult times people are having, they are remembering that with *Perestroika* many positive changes happened in society. It is not a truly democratic society, but important individual rights were gained which the people had never experienced. One of those was the freedom of assembly.

Before the change there was only one political party—the Communist Party. Now there are nearly 100 parties. Before there were very few voluntary, non-political organizations, and now there are more than 15,000. There are more than twenty women's organizations alone. They had neither the right to assemble in protest nor to strike, but now it is an every day occurrence. They watch how Americans and others do things on CNN.

The Russians are acting from example and fit the model to their own needs. Before the change the people had no right to disagree with any action of the party or government. If anyone were accused of undermining the political system of the country, it was a punishable crime.

Officially, religion was never banned, but a large number of churches were closed, and the buildings used for more practical purposes. No one was permitted to sell religious literature and weddings in churches were frowned upon. All church activities were supervised by the secret police. Now there is a renaissance of worship services. Since 1988 hundreds of churches have reopened their doors, and thousands of people attend services. There are sixteen active denominations. Many people want to search independently for their spirituality. Under new laws in Russia any religious organization must have been there for seven years to be recognized as an official church. After being recognized, the church members may distribute their literature and hold services which are open to the public. The Russian Orthodox Church is concerned about so many different sects coming into the country. They call it a spiritual bazaar, and warn of the pitfalls involved. The church is trying to convince the laity to choose the Russian religion which has served the people for over a thousand years.

After the war in Afghanistan ended many Soviet military men were left behind as prisoners of war. After a number of years some have been liberated through state negotiations, but it has caused a dilemma in some families because they came home having accepted Islam as their religion. When they would go through their routine of prayers, it was disturbing to their mothers and other members of their families. Some of the prisoners refused to come back because they wanted to stay and practice their new found religion. They had never worshipped as Soviet citizens, but they had found something as prisoners in Afghanistan that changed their lives. The men began returning home after 1989 when everything was changing in their native country. Russians are not accustomed to being different so Islam was hard to accept for families who had replaced religion with Communism for so many years.

For so many years travel was something Russians could only dream about. A small number of screened persons traveled abroad on business serving the state only with the endorsement of the Central Committee and after being given a list of the rules of behavior while abroad. It was also necessary to get clearance from the KGB.

A few Soviets could travel as tourists, but they were mostly limited to the countries of East Europe. They had to get a foreign travel passport and turn it in as soon as they returned. In 1994 the state decided to give every citizen a foreign passport. For the first few months people stood in long lines for many hours to receive one. In four months four million people got their passports even though only one million of them could afford to travel. Now millions travel abroad for many reasons—research, business, pleasure, or to participate in international forums. Special one week shopping tours into neighboring countries became popular, and in 1997 Yeltsin signed a decree whereby even homeless people could get a passport.

Even though the Soviets had struggled against human rights during the conference which led to the Helsinki Accords of 1975, better rules were established to allow official immigration. Now thousands have immigrated. At first it was mostly Jews going to Israel. Later many immigrated to France, Germany, and the United States. Now that the procedure has become much easier fewer people want to immigrate.

Throughout the years of Soviet power there was only one candidate's name on the ballot in elections. Leadership was hand picked, and the candidate was endorsed by the Central Committee. In 1989 millions of people rushed to the polls to see and participate in an election where there were dozens of candidates for one position. It was such a novelty for the Russians to realize that their vote could make a difference. It was interesting to see candidates preparing their campaign programs.

Another major difference since 1985 is the right to own private property. When the Communist Party was in power owning private property was against the law. Many people cannot cope with the idea, but the rich now own their own property. Up to the present no laws have been passed to allow ownership of the land, but buildings, appliances, furniture stores, and food shops can be privately owned. All along the Volga River cruise between Moscow and St.

Petersberg beautiful *dachas* have been built by these suddenly wealthy individuals where before there were very small, unimpressive buildings. Laws are now needed about the purchase of land.

Looking at the way their lives have changed over a very few years, the Russians now feel that for the first time they can really use their own initiative. They can join organizations of their choice, worship as they please, and correspond with friends and relatives abroad knowing that the letters will not be censored or destroyed. They can receive, without censure, packages, literature, clothes, humanitarian aid, and gifts. Now they can call anywhere in the world from their home phones, whereas before they had to go to the central telegraph office to make calls in order to get through.

Many Russians now use the internet and have E-mail at home. It is all available, but under the present financial conditions the majority of the population cannot afford these conveniences.

The radio stations are no longer jammed so people can hear news from any place in the world. They are unrestrained in their efforts to learn what is, and has been, happening in the world outside of Russia. For the first time they can also sign contracts outside the country without penalty or restraint. When the people go shopping they may select chairs, food, clothing, furniture, TV sets, and high tech equipment from all over the world. Zoya was interviewed by a Japanese television crew who paid her $200. She could and did buy a Japanese television set.

On the cultural side things have also changed drastically. There are many more theaters, and the people can see productions by authors who were previously banned. They hear bands which were not allowed to come in during Communist control. José Carerras has even given a performance in Red Square. Now they can have the exhibits of artists who were labeled dissident and thrown out of the country. The first few years after the ban was lifted theaters were packed by Russians who wanted to see trashy American movies. Now there is a demand for better quality movies. Video is thriving, but some of it is black market.

McDonald's, Kentucky Fried Chicken, and Pizza Hut flourish in the larger cities. To the surprise of foreign visitors, long lines formed at McDonald's when it first opened in the center of Moscow. The chain has contracts with state and private farms for its produce and beef. As people had heard and read about McDonald's they were curious to taste the company's products. Foreign visitors were surprised that the line waiting to get into McDonald's was much longer than the line waiting at Lenin's tomb. This was a first for Moscow!

For many years everyone was about equal in income except a small circle of party bosses. The right to make decisions, and the responsibility that goes with it, is almost too much of a challenge for many citizens who have not been permitted to make decisions for themselves. It makes them vulnerable, depressed, and humiliated. Mentally they are having difficulty coping with the things that are in their favor, but for which they have had no experience or the requisite training to understand. They had read about the changes for a long time, but when they became reality and affected their every day life, they realized that they did not know how to take care of their needs. Coping has become a big challenge for the majority of the people.

The change to a non-Communist society so quickly meant that there was no solid political, economic, or financial ground upon which it was built. These conditions gave rise to currency manipulation, financial speculation, and dealing in illegal money transactions. Quick money made by some found its way into foreign banks.

Crime has rapidly and visibly increased. There are many criminal organizations—similar to the Mafia—fighting and killing for power. The grab for money and transferral of it out of the country continued steadily while the people sank deeper into poverty, uncertainty, and chaos. It is little wonder that they are disillusioned and depressed. They had vision and idealism under Communist Party rule with limited rights. Now they have no vision. Providing for themselves and their families has become a burden.

New laws are needed to fight the expanding monopolies and to protect and improve the lives of over thirty-five million pensioners. Statutory reform is also needed for the military, turning it into a strong , well-organized, professional group. Compulsory conscription must end so that young men can be given a chance to make their own decisions.

Work has just been started simplifying tax laws to make them operational. There were so many loopholes and so much unfairness, that it became impossible to collect taxes from the growing number of new companies. The state cannot take care of the populace in a country collecting only fifty percent of taxes which are due and sorely needed.

The information in this chapter is based on Zoya's experience and knowledge of her changing world. It is difficult to evaluate what happens in all areas of a country as large and well populated as Russia, but living day to day in the midst of it, having contact with high officials, traveling inside and outside the country, and working with a variety of conferences, has given her a wide perspective. She sympathizes with the people and suffers with them.

CHAPTER 14

"And Even After"

BEFORE ZOYA LEFT AUSTIN, Texas, to return to Moscow in 1996, she had a call from a long-standing friend and an experienced former Intourist guide, Zina Petrashova, telling Zoya that she had become the director of the cruise ship *Rus*. She wanted to commit Zoya to lectures on the cruises between Moscow and St. Petersberg. Foreign tourists would be interested in learning all they could from someone with experience. They were anxious to hear more about Russia's history, current political scene, lifestyles and the plight of its people. Zoya agreed to accept the challenge, but she had commitments for some of the cruise dates. Instead she suggested that her daughter, Tatyana, take the alternate cruises.

Zoya got back to Moscow on May 15 and in two days was lecturing aboard the *Rus*. After her first ninety minute lecture, the passengers followed her around on the ship to ask further questions. After listening to the local guides at the various historical ports along the Volga River, they would gather around Zoya because she could give them information about the history of the Volga Region.

This gave her the opportunity to talk about her work for numerous charities for children, the disabled, and the elderly. She spoke of the unlimited needs of this unfortunate segment of the population, and the lack of state support. Many of the tourists responded immediately with monetary gifts. Understanding the high cost of all medication and vitamins, they would send large boxes of over-the-counter medications when they returned to their homes. Zoya, in turn, forwarded the packages to the children of Chechnya, the elderly, the disabled, the lonely with no one to be aware of their needs, and former teachers who do not get their meager pensions on a regular basis. Zoya continued to alternate lectures with her daughter, Tatyana, in 1997 and 1998 and will probably continue to lecture on the cruises as long as she is able to do it.

She receives many letters of appreciation from those who hear her lecture on the ship. But their statements of understanding are the most rewarding. One woman's letter states: "You have certainly given me a new perspective on the people of your country and I wish that all of the people of my country could hear what you have to say. As a nation, we just do not understand the Russian people." Others wrote, "You have made us understand your country and its people and just how much the secrecy and control of the leaders of the country have set the base for world opinion. This is true of all major country leaders, but we have heard more of the negative attitudes about your country. Thank you for telling it as it is."

But perhaps these attitudes are best expressed in a poem Jerry Roth wrote on June 23, 1998, while aboard the cruise ship.

> A voyage profounder than was promised
>   Through a countryside older than time,
> Home to a people of smiling sorrows
>   Whose belltowers never chime.
>
> We sail down alleys of dark green forest
>   Sprinkled with church domes that gleam in white night
> Inside are troves of gilded icons
>   Dead souls of millions in each candle's light.
>
> We wander down streets paved with granite
>   In the outsized footsteps of bloodthirsty tsars
> Who left their people a legacy of terror and greatness
>   And now a millenium of brutal scars.

In magnificent artwork, portraits and landscapes
   By painters whose names we were never taught
Ilya Repin and Alexander Ivanov
   The eternal life of a nation it wrought.

We see birch trees dipped in silver
   Rainswept lakes that stretch like seas
Hilltop forts with woodcarved chapels
   A Kremlin throne for tsars decrees.

Greeted ashore by wrinkled babushkas
   Wilted flowers, toothless smiles,
Small boys proudly hawking postcards
   Their sisters strutting girlish styles.

We see soldiers marching brusquely
   Armed with swagger and with guns
But their smooth faces betray them
   As nothing more than boys—our sons.

And I stop and I wonder that for the past fifty years
   Our arrows have been pointed at these people's hearts.
Missiles aimed at Moscow—the Kremlin and the children
   That guide in Yaroslavl; those peasants pushing carts.

And I commit to myself each day that I'm here
   I'll look long and deeply into one Russian's eyes
And celebrate jointly that we have outlasted
     the war clouds
And begun to uncover those old human ties.

In the fall of 1996 Great Britain sent a television crew to Russia to shoot a documentary on the Cold War. They had chosen a number of war veterans and prominent political figures of the era for interviews. Zoya was asked to talk about her experiences and feelings about World War II and the follow-up period. This documentary has been showing on CNN starting in 1998 and continues to be shown.

The international organization "Educators for Peace and Understanding" celebrated its tenth anniversary in February 1998. It was held in the capitol of the now independent state of Belarus-

Minsk. Many former republics of the Soviet Union, now independent states, sent their delegates. There were also delegations from
affiliated organizations in France and from Accent on Understanding. There were workshops on the problems faced by educators in
these difficult times of change. Zoya was pleased that the organization she founded was continuing to serve as an advocate for peace
and still attracted members from so many different geographical
areas.

Moscow celebrated its 850th anniversary September 5-6, 1997.
Zoya and some of her colleagues visited schools and youth sports
centers and told the students about their experiences during and
after World War II. They reminisced about the great celebration of
the 800th anniversary of Moscow in 1947. Later when they went to
city hall, they were decorated with the 850 year commemorative
medal.

A special television crew asked Zoya to participate in a documentary, *Behind the Scenes of the War.* The plans were to document
the role of Soviet Intelligence during the conferences in Tehran,
Yalta, and Potsdam where she had worked as the only female intelligence officer during World War II. She was able to share information that had not been known before and suggested that they see
the special section related to these conferences in the World War II
Museum. She knew that there they would see the table and chairs
which she and her assistant had ordered custom made as a "wedding
present" from one of the furniture shops in the city of Tehran.

It was not until October 1998 when she saw the documentary
in Great Britain that she learned from Beria's son about his father
bugging the British and American quarters on orders from Stalin
during two of the conferences. Then she realized why Stalin was always so well prepared for discussions with his counterparts throughout the sessions. The script of everything that had been discussed in
the Allied quarters in Yalta was handed to him each day by Beria
before he went into the discussions. Zoya had high clearance and
knew a lot about what was going on, but as she explains it, when you
work in secrecy it also applies from one department to another.

While the documentary was being filmed, the producer
thought Zoya's reminiscences interesting enough to be worthy of a
separate documentary. Her ability to communicate verbally is extra-
ordinary. Little wonder that the producer was impressed. She was

happy to add still unknown incidents and her own personal feelings about the events during the conferences. The date for showing it has not been set.

During Moscow's 850th anniversary celebration Zoya and others worked to put together a children's art festival. They had done this before, but they had more participants this time, including foreign students from five schools that cater to the children of foreign residents stationed in Moscow. They are from Italy, Hungary, India, Germany, and the United States. With money collected from volunteers, they were able to bring eighteen children from Chechnya who were victims of land mines. Their drawings reminded Zoya of terrible scenes of the war in the forties.

While the children were in the city for ten days they saw the sights, attended a performance of *The Nutcracker* ballet at the Bolshoi Theater, and went to Christmas parties. The toys exhibited at the festival were given to the children as they boarded the train to Chechnya. The farewells were touching and very emotional. Sometime later Zoya received an official "Thank you!" letter signed by the Deputy President of the Republic of Chechnya, Mr. Zakaev. In Moscow she received a special medal for organizing activities in the humanitarian field.

In the spring of 1998 the Sports Dynamo Club was celebrating its 75th anniversary. In December 1934 Zoya was one of the founding members of the first youth sports club in the Soviet Union—Young Dynamo. When the club celebrated sixty years of club activity, three of the founders—Belyaev Pavel, world record holder in speed skating; Buchin Victor, the national ski coach; and Zoya, national champion in track and field, were decorated by Yeltsin with a special medal for active participation in the education of Russian youth.

That spring the Dynamo veterans shared their sports and life experiences with young members of the club. The celebration of the event took place in a large sports complex in Moscow. The entire procedure, including congratulations and the closing concert, was nationally televised.

On October 29, 1998, the older generation of Russians were marking eighty years since the founding of the Young Communist League, or Komsomol. It was a great time for them to remember the days of their youth, the glorious dreams they had, and the energy they put into implementing those dreams. As they looked back they could say that they were proud of the years of actively participating in the building of their socialist dreams and of defending Russia during the Nazi invasion. They were also proud of the years of intense work that restored the life of the country and helped heal the wounds for the loss of millions of people who were their fathers, brothers, husbands, and dear ones.

Contemporary Russian youth met this holiday with mixed feelings. Some of them do not even know what it means to be active in implementing a dream. According to Zoya, they are often too pragmatic and devoid of the romanticism that helped her generation through the stressful years. She adds that she is an incorrigible optimist, and she is convinced that things cannot get worse than they are today. She also says that they sang songs at the reunions which they will never forget and will probably keep them young forever!

Zoya was invited to go to Great Britain in October 1998 to initiate sister school contacts in Northern Wales. She visited with old friends, made new ones, and was surprised when people told her that they had seen her in the *Cold War Documentary*. She told them that in the documentary she had been identified as a KGB Colonel, but the truth is that she had retired from the military as a Captain and is just as proud of her service.

When she arrived in the United States in December 1998, many people mentioned the *Cold War Documentary*. She was pleased that Americans are interested in analyzing history, and hopes that we all learn from the mistakes our leaders made during that period. She insists that for the sake of our children and grandchildren, and in the best interest of all, we must rethink our past to make sure that the dreadful times of the Cold War are never repeated.

Of all the important things that may happen for Zoya in 1999, the dearest to her heart is a final decision about issuing a commemorative stamp honoring her father, Vasily Zarubin. Authorities were planning to issue one in 1994 when her father would have been one hundred years old. It was postponed, but now she has been asked to choose a photograph of her father which she would prefer to have on the stamp. She, her brother Peter, and the extended family are happy and proud that he will finally be recognized in this way for his many years of faithful and dedicated service to his country.

Women's organizations in Germany will publish a one-volume collection of biographies of outstanding women from thirty-five countries in Europe. The women chosen will tell their life stories and give advice to young women for the twenty-first century. These preeminent women will share their experiences, frustrations, and dreams. Zoya has been chosen as the outstanding woman of Russia to be included in the book.

She has been working and lecturing at the Diplomatic Academy for more than thirty years, and she enjoys sharing her experience and expertise with younger members of the faculty and the student-diplomats. The Academy will celebrate its sixty-fifth anniversary in the fall of 1999. It is a unique educational establishment that prepares specialists in many fields to serve their country in foreign diplomacy. It also offers short-term refresher courses to keep the diplomats up to date on world affairs.

Zoya's volunteer work is extensive. She has an ongoing interest in developing professional contacts and expanding student exchanges in a number of Moscow schools, particularly Schools Number 20 and 240. The Yurorskaya Boarding School in the Moscow region cares for 110 cerebral palsied children. Zoya visits them and brings much needed multi-vitamins, medicines, clothes, books, and school supplies. She gets emotionally involved, but their needs are so great she continues to do all she can for them. This effort becomes extensive with the help of friends.

"For years my work brought me close to my people who gave me inspiration and strength. When I was abroad, I felt that I was representing my people, and I was fortunate to be chosen by circumstances to be in that position. I knew that I had to do my best. To use an American expression—I was always a mover and shaker. I was brought up to be an optimist, and it has supported me through difficult and tragic times. I live with purpose and have few regrets."

When she relates the most exciting events of her life, she first mentions, Victory Day (May 9, 1945; the end of World War II) as a day of great celebration. The streets were crowded with happy people, and there were fantastic fireworks displays. There was a feeling of elation and looking forward to life with optimism believing that the worst was history.

The second most memorable day was August 1, 1975, the day

in Finlandia Hall when thirty-five heads of states of Europe, the United States, and Canada signed the Helsinki Accords. These ensured stable interstate relations, cooperation in the fields of trade and commerce, and improvement in the controversial field of human rights. This document was nicknamed the Moral Code of Behavior and was the best possible substitute for a peace treaty in the Cold War.

Another landmark day was May 9, 1995, when Russia celebrated the fiftieth anniversary of victory over Fascist Germany. War veterans visited schools, colleges, universities, enterprises, and military troops. The veterans also received a personal letter from President Yeltsin with kind words of appreciation and respect for their participation in bringing about the great victory. As a war veteran, Zoya feels especially privileged to have been a witness to these events that changed the world. She is sure they were brought to fruition in great measure by the peace activists. She is proud to have been a part of, and a moving force behind, these movements throughout the world. She is sad that her husband who was also a war veteran did not live to see the good things happen.

In retrospect Zoya talks about her work as head interpreter as an enriching experience to see, work, and interpret for so many world leaders and Soviet politicians. The work gave her a sense of belonging where so many decisions were made that affected the well-being of the world.

In Russia, the family is a close-knit and dependable unit. The extended family can be large, but they care and keep in touch. Zoya's story would not be complete without mentioning her experience of living in two families. Her beloved mother Olga, who stayed in China with Leonid Eitingon when her husband was recalled to Moscow, was the uniting force in the second family. She pays special tribute to her father, Vasily Zarubin, whom she calls her role model and inspiration. Zoya could never even think of calling his second wife, charming Liza, "step-mother." She was always friendly, supportive, and attentive to Zoya and was her confidante. Nor could she call Leonid Eitingon "step-father." She called him Uncle Leonid. He was a great influence during her formative years, and he never made her feel like a step-daughter. He was always kind and loving. When she was young he took her on some of his special assignments. To Zoya he was an outstanding example of unwavering loyalty to their country.

Since she was brought up in what she calls a "conglomerate family," she talks about her siblings. "Svetlana who was born in China to Olga and Leonid is as close to me as a sister can be, and I never thought of her as a 'half-sister.' She will always be my little sister. She is now retired from the medical profession and helping to care for her two grandsons, Sergei, Jr. and Peter, the children of her daughter Lena and Sergei, Sr., who is a promising new-generation researcher in economics. Svetlana's older son, Leonid, is a new-generation researcher in nuclear physics. Peter Zarubin born in Europe to Zarubin and Liza is as close to me as a brother can be, and we have so much to share.

"In Leonid's former families there were two boys and a girl. Vladimir is the oldest, and has a Ph.D. in economics and is dean of the department at Voronzh University. The second son, Leonid, is a businessman and a proud grandfather; and the daughter, Muza, is an aerobics instructor and the mother of two charming sons. They are all a part of my close-knit extended family.

"My beloved daughter, Tatyana, is a sports journalist who periodically teaches English. Very often I feel guilty because the tragic circumstances in my family kept me from spending enough time with her when she was an adolescent. We have similar interests in politics, theater, and art, and enjoy being together now.

"Alexei, Tatyana's son, graduated from the History Department of Moscow University and studied for a year at James Madison University in Virginia. At the age of twenty-five, he is currently working in a bank which, fortunately, has remained open in Moscow after the financial crash in August 1998. I am proud of some of his achievements, but at times am concerned about his choice of priorities and disinterest in family loyalty and every day responsibilities. I continue to hope that he will mature into being an adult of whom the family will be proud. Changes are inevitable in the present generation.

"My late husband's daughter, Stella, is an English language teacher at the Lumumba University in Moscow. Tatyana and Stella are very good friends and to the surprise of many call each other 'sister.' Recently, she told me that she had never thought of me as a 'step-mother' because I had always been so much more than that. Her husband, Dolya, is an engineer.

"With all I have related about my family, you can easily understand what we mean by an extended family in Russia. As attitudes change in the world, I can only hope that close family relations remain the same in my country."

The ultimate purpose in writing this book is the hope that in telling the life story of one Russian woman who has run the gamut of tragedy, success, and recognition it will help those who have known so little about the human stories in the Soviet Union and Russia. Zoya's story shows that whatever happens to Russia and her people over the next twenty-five or thirty years will affect the rest of the people in the world.

Index